' REALITY OF LIFE '

a collection of poetry and song lyrics, published four times by "the International Library of Poetry" as one of the best poems and poets of the 20th century, I am in their historical archives as poets elite.

Written by

Steven morehu Davies.

From New Zealand.

'Aotearoa', Polynesian 'maori' name for NZ.

****

ISBN : 9-781791-788971.

If any person or musical artists are interested in recording any of my top quality written song lyrics, you are most welcome to contact me on

(steven.davies.publishing@gmail.com)

thank you,

Steven morehu Davies,

famous poet and song lyricist.

" DEDICATIONS "

3

I Dedicate this book to the following people for there support over the years.

Eydie (honey-rosebud) Morehu,
Araiteuru Morehu
Te Mapu Morehu,
Ian Kenneth Davies,
Wayne Halliday,
Jimmy (jocks) Davies,
Michelle (shell) Davies,
Shontelle (shony) Davies/Hughes.
Josephine (josie) Davies,
Ritchie (luey) Davies,
Sharon Areta Davies/Rameka,
Andrew (conch) Davies,
Jason Halliday,
Tyrone Halliday,
Deserae Halliday/Mrkusich,
Aroha Tautau/Malton,
Hinera Tautau/Wade,
Nikora Tautau/Curtis,
Graham Tautau,

Chris Tautau/Morgan,
KevinTautau,
Carmen (Bianca) Wade/Horan,
Ricky (Ducky) Morehu,
Gwen Morehu,
Patricia Tito,
Cheryl Tito/Stephens,
Hoani Ranui,
Colin Mihaka,
Susanne (tootsy) Grooby,
Colleen (Mamma dear) Grooby,
Dr Danette Grooby,
Christine Grooby
Grant Grooby,
Emmalisa Hoani.

" ACKNOWLEDGEMENTS "

I would like to show my gratitude to my mother Eydie who passed away due to a long illness who would always show continued interest and steadfast support and faith in my writings over my lifetime, she always encouraged me to keep writing even through difficult times in my life and she was there to strengthen me, a truly precious person indeed.

I would also like to do the same for my closest beloved lost cousin Aroha Tautau/Malton who always showed constant interest in my poetry, and would tell many people about my work with much praise, along with the rest of the Tautau family.

I thank my old girlfriend Emmalisa Hoani for her advice, support and encouragement to help get my poetry published.

Also a big thank you to many of my close cousins and family in the dedications who always spoke highly of my works over the years.

And last but not least, to my closest and dearest friend Susanne Grooby of the past twenty years for her dedicated companionship and strengthening support through our tragic mental health issues we faced, struggles and sufferings on low benefit income.

" INTRODUCTION "

I am Steven Morehu Davies, I was published in 2000 in an anthology with just over one thousand other poets worldwide, by 'The International Library of Poetry' titled 'memories of the millennium' 'the best poems and poets of the 20th century', as printed on the hardbound cover book in gold embossed lettering, with my poem titled 'awaiting arms', I had achieved instant recognition for my writing talent when I submitted my first poem 'the lonely wanderer' in 1999 in an anthology titled 'fire in the heart', I was further published again in 2001 with my poem titled 'rainbow freckles' in 'the best poems of 2001', and then in 1996 my 3 poems were then selected and published in a 250 page anthology called 'imortal verses series', I stopped submitting in 2002 after an upsetting relationship breakup, unfortunate indeed, to positive things, I am listed in their historical archives as poets elite, I have been writing in my spare time around 38 years, and in this poetry collection is a selection of my works, namely 'edition one'.

Two reasons why I love to write poetry.

   Firstly-, I like the challenge of finding from the vast dictionary of words available that rhyme in harmony with what I am expressing, usually the last word of first and second line together, and the third and fourth line together, in paragraphs of frequently 4 lines throughout each poem, very often I also like to create a constant and unique structure pattern throughout each poem as well, since I am a thorough writer and cover much detail, then sometimes the lines can be lengthy and I feel it reads more fluently and sounds better that way if read aloud, most of the time I also tend to try to end the very last word or words to correspond with the actual 'title' of the poem itself, I think it gives it a more powerful impact and statement that way, and makes my writing more dramatic indeed.

   Secondly-, I love the idea of having the freedom to express my emotions and opinions about society and the world we all inhabit and contribute towards somehow and in some way, I like to write about truth and fact, the reality of the way things actually are, mainly human sufferings, hardships, redundancy, being on low income and struggling on low government benefit, keeping law abiding as citizens, and trying all sorts of ways to make ends meet by striving to raise a young family, my attitude and out look towards society may seem negative and critical, but a lot of my poetry are from personal experiences or what I have seen and heard about from radio, the daily news, television and newspapers.
Many thousands of people have experienced sufferings in some way, either emotionally, psychologically, physically or financially, I do hope that my writings will give people a 'sigh of relief ' or maybe gladden you in heart and spirit knowing that sufferings affect all people from all walks of life, weather rich or poor, for me as a low income earner and many others, it is the hurtful pains of making no headway, and the desires to be occupied in the work place earning self satisfaction pride of providing a comfortable and happy life style for their children, it is to all those people whom I dedicate this book,
Money is a priority and essential to provide our basic needs, the truth is that after many years of trying and struggling, people end up with 'I have had enough' or 'I can not take this anymore' attitude, not having enough money to achieve goals eventually builds up and causes severe friction, tension and strain on the family often leading to crime, domestic violence, court hearings, prison terms, child abuse, separations and divorce, sadly, New Zealand has one of the most highest suicide rates for

young people in the world, I myself have been hearing voices on and off for around 25 years and have attempted suicide 3 times, I strongly believe that some voices are very supportive and some are evil, the slander that I received was unbearable and I believe that I was saved by an unknown higher realm due to my earlier on going prayers and bible studies, in the late 1800s the 'bible students' now call 'Jehovah witnesses' on their studies published an article in the newspaper concluding that 1914 would be a turning point in mankinds history, on their calculations of the 'gentile times',as a result 'world war one' occurred that year, and that war had broke out in heaven and the great dragon 'satan the devil' was hurled down to earth with one third of the angels whom turned rebellious and became demons, and that god has set a date to end all unrighteousness on earth with armageddon, while his son jesus christ is setting up a righteous government and at the same time sorting out the sheeplike ones from the goats as explained in the bible, after armageddon there is a 1000 year 'judgement day' in which during that time the dead would be resurrected back to life with gods holy spirit, and they will have the opportunity to except gods righteousness, also while the earth is restored back to it's original paradise conditions, during that 1000 years the devil and his demons would be put in prison and released again for a little while to tempt mankind a final time, then finally annihilated,- I am not here to preach in this poetry publication but I needed to explain what I have learnt over the years, and I personaly think that is the reason for all the troubles mankind has faced and also the reason why I was hearing wicked spirits myself.

Often people do not seek help or counselling and their anxiety is released on prostitution, alcohol and drugs to help ease pressure, instead of being a temporary relaxation it easily becomes a regular routine, a vicious daily or weekly cycle and eventually an addiction not managing to pay basic necessities like rents, mortgages, electricity bills, maintenance, court fines and providing food on the table, with an empty fridge and cupboards, suddenly they are faced with reminder notices, higher interest charges, overdue accounts and tenancy evictions, with no money flooding in to help and no where to go, the pressure is unbearable and it is usually the children who pay the innocent cost.

A very sad but true reality of our inherited imperfections and sins, as there are no perfect humans anywhere on earth today, and it seems to be always trying and trying attitude and learning from our mistakes most of the time, especially in our day and age of economic global climate, seems to me that life is associated with a desire to succeed, trial and error and still a will to show love and have forgiveness.

Steven morehu davies.

" POETRY COLLECTIONS "

1/.   The world is this book.
2/.   Awaiting arms.
3/.   Our creators image.
4/.   Can you teach me to live on forever.
5/.   Sometimes.
6/.   The loner.
7/.   The drifter.
8/.   Mean machine.
9/.   Anxiety.
10/.   The dole.
11/.   Breath of life.
12/.   The lonely wanderer.
13/.   The fallen leaf.
14/.   As I sleep on again tonight.
15/.   Forevermore.
16/.   No red letter year.
17/.   Maturity of age.
18/.   Just yesterday.
19/.   Root of all evil.
20/.   Armageddon.
21/.   When I'm insane.
22/.   Rags to riches.
23/.   The joker.
24/.   The joker in the pack.
25/.   The new world.
26/.   The refugee.

27/. The unknown hour.
28/. Imperfection.
29/. Hello and goodbye.
30/. The midnight butt stroller.
31/. Not leaving me with death.
32/. Just one beer.
33/. The contented bottle.
34/. Quiet drink.
35/. Still I seek it somemore.
36/. So confused.
37/. Silverdream.
38/. Castle of gold.
39/. Civilised state.
40/. Planet earth.
41/. Back into my life.
42/. Silverdream.
43/. Castle of gold.
44/. Growing child.
45/. Monarchs in the yard.
46/. Rainbow freckles.
47/. The gold treasure chest.
48/. Grandmothers photo.
49/. The bond key.
50/. Hey mum !, still the best.
51/. Jimmy (jocks) james.
52/. My dear michelle.
53/. My baby shontelle.
54/. Rarotongan josie.
55/. Chevara (shell).

56/. Out of it sue.
57/. Dear sue.
58/. For my girl.
59/. Uncle joe.
60/. Dan the man.
61/. Angel sue.
62/. Down underground.
63/. Tom and june.
64/. Sweet honey flower.
65/. Huru and mapu (never ever surrender).
66/. Gardeners daughter.
67/. The tenderest kiss.
68/. Girl called jade.
69/. Clairvoyance (for maria).
70/.   Awhina darlena.

Three anthology books published by 'the international library of poetry'.
1999-- 'fire in the heart', poem 'the lonely wanderer'.
2000-- 'memories of the millennium' 'best poems and poets of the 20th century', poem 'awaiting arms'
2001-- 'best poems and poets of 2001' poem, 'rainbow freckles'.

'Reality of Life'   Steven morehu Davies

Photograph
taken 1st day
of the
'millennium'
1st january
2000.

15

'Reality of Life'   Steven morehu Davies

'Reality of Life'   Steven morehu Davies

'Reality of Life'   Steven morehu Davies

" the world is this book " copyright by steven morehu
davies, completed 17 april 1995.

I wrote these life's poems,
From my heart it still bleeds,
Life's reality I have have shown,
For the whole world to read.

I wrote these life's poems,
From survival times of poor,
Life's daily struggles are known,
For the whole world can't ignore.

I wrote these life poems,
From my sole personal view,
Life's weaknesses have strength grown,
For the whole world I knew.

I wrote these life poems,
From withdrawal times of spare,
Life's humble ones I owe them,
For the whole world to share.

I wrote these life poems,
From non christian activity,
Life's divine prophecies are open,
For the whole world is in captivity.

 I wrote these life poems,
From life's trials I have spent,
Life's heavenly purposes have spoken,
For the whole world must repent.

I wrote these life poems,
From my biblical interest outlook,
Life's imperfect spiritual omen,
For the whole world is this book.

" awaiting arms " copyright by steven morehu davies,
completed 18 february 1999, chorus 27 may 2012.

I see the wonderful moist complexion,
of your distinct olive coloured face,
The mature shape of virgin innocence,
dressed up in purest ribbon and lace,
So beautiful and true gracious,
in light of the purest crimson skies,
as it sparkles genuine pureness,
in your staring crystal hazel eyes.

I see a magnificent crowned princess,
with an appearance of honesty grand,
The freedom of life's gentle breeze,
warms up the cool million golden sands,

So vivid and true displayed,
behind view of sparkling waterfall peaks,
as lips of soft pastel cherry,
blend into your young and tender cheeks.

(chorus)

You are my dignity,
You are my awaiting arms,
You are the woman,
I'll never do you any harm,
You are my loyalty,
nothing will tear us apart,
You are the woman,
you are the love of my heart.

I imagine a woman,
just like you in my mind,
I believe because,
love is so hard to find,
I just wish it would be,
the way that it all seems,
because you are the woman,
the only woman of my dreams.

I see a woman of prime curved nudity,
in an historic portrait of fearless wonder,
The side profile of quietened moments,
in a timeless and poetic ponder,

So restful and true feminine,
you stretch across the great and wide divide,
As tranquil emotions reflect real feelings,
that a true woman can never hide.

I see a glamorous smile just glowing,
amongst the flickering great distant stars,
The mirror of all artistic creations,
flowing within heavenly clouds up afar,
So dignified and true peaceful,
in pride of mother earth's life giving soils,
As aromas of personal devotions,
blends perfumes of your incensed chosen oils.

I see your splendid image like satin,
in the close encounter of moonlighting shade,
The fragrance of new spring flowers,
as the sunset doves flight in gradual fade,
So generous and true inviting,
as your hair flows free like blue waters of calm,
As the millennium horizon connects us,
we melt into each others eternal, awaiting arms.

" our creators image " copyright by steven morehu davies,
completed 3 december 1995.

This miracle human body with perfect features all in one,
We look and we see,
Our eyes view the light moon and the bright sun,

We sniff and we smell,
Our nose senses many aroma so beautifully well,
We hear and we listen,
Our ears are designed that of echo seashell.

We touch and we feel,
Our thumbs designed to have control independence,
We rove and we taste,
Our tongues have pleasure delight of soul repentance,
We think and we wonder,
Our minds imagine ideas of convenient flexibility,
We stand and we walk,
Our feet balance our regular everyday mobility.

We bite and we chew,
Our teeth grind down revealing marvelous flavours,
We desire and we love,
Our genitals connect for our sexual behaviours,
We speak and we talk,
Our mouths communicate in together conversation,
We learn and we know,
Our brain concentrates on our future organisation.

We nibble and we suck,
Our breasts hold milk for new born nourishment,
We rest and we sleep,
Our soul conscience of yearning waking encouragement,

We tire and we sit,
Our bottom is cushioned releasing uncomfortable grief,
We occupy and we work,
Our hands busy with self satisfaction employment relief.

We act and we try,
Our muscles function with every possible incline,
We comb and we present,
Our hair decoration beautifies our outstanding design,
We dress and we appear,
Our clothes fashion reflects moods personal decision,
We blink and we view,
Our eye lashes reject dust for clear focus precision.

We pulse and we live,
Our heartbeat delivers the key to intention desire,
We eat and we survive,
Our natural instinct to intake the food that we require,
We understand and we value,
Identifying ourselves for contribution satisfaction,
We learn and we skill,
Personal interests progress for people intereaction,

We experience and we share,
Emotional tears burst out as we hurtfully cry,
We marry and we bond,
Coupled vows remain in trusted connection until we die,

We breed and we cherish,
Family raising at our best within imperfect frustration,
We live and we honour,
Gods image we do pride within his free gifted creation.

" can you teach me to live on forever " copyright by
steven morehu davies, completed 17 april 1995.

Mamma, can you train me how to suckle your warm
breast,
Mamma, can you train me how to sleep tender warm rest,
Mamma, can you train me how to call out for your heart,
Mamma, can you train me how to make a happy new start.

Mamma, can you teach me how to roll over and crawl,
Mamma, can you teach me how to lean against the wall,
Mamma, can you teach me how to stand steady and walk,
Mamma, can you teach me all the new baby alphabet talk.

Mamma, can you teach me to be an infant so sweet,
Mamma, can you show me the open paradise wheat,
Mamma, can you teach me to clean up our nice house,
Mamma, can you teach me how to be a really nice spouse.

Mamma, can you teach me to do all things all so right,
Mamma, can you show me the lovely christmas snow
white,
Mamma, can you teach me how to kick far a big giant ball,
Mamma, can you teach me how to grow strong and real
tall.

Mamma, can you teach me how do autumn leaves show,
Mamma, can you show me the colourful skies rainbow,
Mamma, can you teach me how to have lots of money,
Mamma, can you teach me how to be beautiful like honey.

Mamma, can you teach me to behave at my very best,
Mamma, can you show me a real lifes new birds nest,
Mamma, can you teach me god's natural cycle plan,
Mamma, can you teach me how to be a good gentleman.

Mum, can you teach me all the things not to forget,
Mum, can you show me the sparkling seashore sunset,
Mum, can you teach me how does feminine maturity grow,
Mum, can you teach me all the wise things that you know.

Dad, can you teach me how we were so wonderfully made,
Dad, can you show me the reflecting moonlighting shade,
Dad, can you teach me to grow up real wise and clever,
Dad, can you teach me how we can all live on forever.

" sometimes " copyright by steven morehu davies,
completed 15 april 1997.

Sometimes, you will feel hurt deep within your warm
heart,
Sometimes, you will want to make a fresh brand new
start,
Sometimes, you will think you have progressed on so
well,
Sometimes, you will be put through just sheer bloody hell.

Sometimes, you will feel hurt deep into your very bones,
Sometimes, you will lose your only old haven rest home,
Sometimes, you will lose your very true kids and your
ring,
Sometimes, you will blink and then lose your everything.

Sometimes, you will be hurt deep in through your very
veins,
Sometimes, you will struggle real hard to get out of the
pains,
Sometimes, you may think you maybe a born millionaire,
Sometimes, you you will be robbed of your every share.

Sometimes, you will be bloody well angry deep down
inside,
Sometimes, you just want to be all alone and just to hide,
Sometimes, you will do really nasty things you don't
mean,
Sometimes, you will simply hate everything you have
been.

Sometimes, you will always suffer then fall into deep love,
Sometimes, you will simply curse our creator god up
above,
Sometimes, you will be totally confused and wonder just
why,
Sometimes, you will just break apart and bloody well cry.

Sometimes, you will always suffer then fall into deep love,
Sometimes, you will simply curse our creator god up
above,
Sometimes, you will be totally confused and wonder just
why,
Sometimes, you will just break apart and bloody well cry.

Sometimes, you will always feel mistreated and unfairly
abused,
Sometimes, you will feel you have just been rubbished and
used,
Sometimes, you will ponder back on memories that have
past,
Sometimes, you will simply dwell on pity that should of
last.

Sometmes, you will want to go out there only just to kill,
Sometimes, you will choose suicide as your only true will,
Sometimes, you will feel guilty of some stupid sinful
shame,
Sometimes, you will simply look for someone imperfect to
blame.

Sometimes, you will do evil things and get foolishly drunk,
Sometimes, you will want to go out and flirt with any old
spunk,
Sometimes, you will just bloody give up and don't care
anymore,
Sometimes, you will want to sleep around with any cheap
whore.

Sometimes, you will want to change your personality into another,
Sometimes, you will truly love then turn against your own mother,
Sometimes, you will want to change your crying babies nappy,
Sometimes, you will long for true love and simply want to be happy.

Sometimes, you will search for answers and hope to just understand,
Sometimes, you will want to grab hold of scared enemies lost hand,
Sometimes, you will simply believe the world is getting worse by the day,
Sometimes, you will see us mankind just suffering in every way.

Sometimes, you will need to talk to a friend who will only listen,
Sometimes, you will wonder if the bible is real or only a suspicion,
Sometimes, you will just need to talk to a real friend who will hear,
Sometimes, you will really wonder if gods Armageddon is nearly near.

Sometimes, you took care of me and I was so bible bloody blind,
Sometimes, god created you for me, you are so easy, not so hard not to find,

Sometimes, I am evil and I sinned to you with some stupid
old crime,
Sometimes, we both only know, that the world turns
around everytime,
but for us, maybe today, again today, just maybe
'sometimes'.

" the loner " copyright by steven morehu davies,
completed 14 september 1993.

Quiet, lonely and shy,
the man kept to himself,
Passing most of his time,
drifting around and about.

Only has himself to depend,
he rarely sees his real mother,
He ain't got many friends,
he ain't got any lover.

He don't trust anyone,
he's been broken and cheated,
He's never had much fun,
always hurt and mistreated.

Feelings for his old girl,
he just keeps himself going,
Where he will end in this world,
he has no way of knowing.

Taking the pain night and day,
striving on year after year,
Nothing gets in his way,
he does not sense any fear.

Back out into the dim moon,
trying to hold his control,
His guitar strikes out a deep tune,
reflecting his powerful soul.

(chorus)

He's the loner, drifting into the night,
He's the loner, searching for the light,
He's the loner, he's just one of a kind,
He's the loner, trying to find his mind,

He's the loner, searching for a new start,
He's the loner, trying to find his heart,
He's the loner, searching for his goals,
He's the loner, trying to find his soul.

Theres no time for good rest,
the journeys rough and long,
He faces lifes ultimate tests,
he changes pain into song.

Upon his every long stride,
his past cutting him deep,
Nothing left there inside,
worn out hungry and weak.

With the heavy load on his back,
the wet strain in his feet,
The man dressed in black,
is back onto the street.

His guitar can't escape lying,
he don't want any owner,
His self esteem keeps on dying,
and this man is the loner.

" the drifter " copyright by steven morehu davies,
completed 22 january 1998, chorus completed 2012.

He's just a drifter, he's just so poor,
Where he's going, he's just so unsure,
Walking the city streets, and the old roads,
With no firm destiny, or any fixed abode.

He's just a drifter, he's just so lost,
Roaming the paths, at the lowest cost,
He wonders around, with a confused mind,
With no definite place, out there to find.

He's just a drifter, he's just so lonely,
Previous years had given, him struggles only,
He possesses motivation, that's just so slow,
With no sure or certain, of any home to go.

(chorus)

The drifter, drifting out there all alone,
The drifter, drifting further away from home,
The drifter, don't know where or ever knowing,
The drifter, don't know on earth he is going,

The drifter, he's never knowing of where he will be,
The drifter, just a lost wood on the rough sea,
The drifter, trying hard not to go insane,
The drifter, just drifting, all alone once again.

He's just a drifter, he's just so trying,
Missing his children, he denies that he's crying,
Taking travelling work, when and wherever he can,
With no guidance, for this young poor man.

He's just a drifter, he's so in strife,
Longing to reunite, his hurting wedded life,
He plans to rectify, those old bonded things,
With desperate feelings, about his little offspring.

He's just a drifter, he's just in disgrace,
Desires to return home, to his family's place,
He arrived back to share, a warm christmas night,
With intentions, of doing all things right.

He's just a drifter, he's just so alone,
Finances force's him again, to leave the old home,
He hugs his small kids, in a raged fired pain,
With shattered goals, he walks back out again.

He's just a drifter, he's just so slow,
Where he's going to now, he just does not know,
This worn lonely drifter, only chose to travel back home,
But sadly again, he's just a drifter, once again, all alone.

" mean machine " copyright by steven morehu davies,
completed 13 december 1994.

Clear away, move aside, race time, mean machine,
Shelby mustang, custom style, silver wheels, ladies mean,
Fats spinning, power honey, steaming mamma, displaying show,
Lake pipes, pumping smoke, ready steady, burns to go.

Gathered glimpse, towns folk, black knight, hits the town,
Scattered bare, danger street, killer queen, seizing her ground,
Whispering beware, shivers behold, hungry block, the pistons heat,
Silent dead, ghostly peeps, idling centre, of empty street.

Faces stunned, blinded flash, visions shine, her body chrome,
Rival fright, dreaded shame, thirsty throttle, is full home,
Roaring blasts, purple gas, concert volume, of pounding amps,
Pretty model, hot rod art, custom paint, shows off tank.

(chorus)

Watch out !, she's the mean machine,
She's the power machine,
She's the meanest honey,
You've ever seen,
Beware !, she's ready in line,
She's bursting this time,
She'll take you blind,
Yes !, every single time,
Beware !, she'll take your head !
She's the power dread,
She'll take you to bed,
She's my blow away Jon Lord,
My blow away Henry Ford !

She'll take you're head,
Whenever she's red,
Beware !, she'll steal your ground,
She's the best around,
She'll steal your heart,
She'll tear you apart !

Watch out !, she's the mean machine,
She's the meanest honey,
you've ever seen!

Thunder strikes, lightning volts, slightest touch, of
trembling pedal,
Rubber fumes, raised trunk, breaks released, of screeching
metal,

Earth tremors, rattling vibration, vicious venom, of awesome might,
Vanished bass, seconds flat, invisible rocket, out of sight.

Display freeway, heatwave straight, noise levels, revs in top,
Open highway, sound barrier, victory speed, she's won't stop,
Warning signs, stinger bee, backfire echo, is flooded wet,
Increased pace, intense heat, lethal stream, of danger jet.

Poison overdrive, inspired fear, grasping proud, her front load,
Majestic cruise, magical ease, monster carves, up waiting road,
Showroom diamond, mint perfection, luxury classic, of glitter sheen,
Priceless gem, deadly cool, lustrous black, the mean machine.

" anxiety " copyright by steven morehu davies, completed 21 december 1996.

I wake up in this brand new day,
search ing for that better way,
More problems I seem to find,
uneasiest of the troubled mind.

'Reality of Life'   Steven morehu Davies

I wake up in this brand new day,
working towards a more generous pay,
More worries seem to be found,
just enough to pull you back down.

I wake up in this brand new day,
building up dreams on what I say,
More barriers I just seem to face,
stumbling over so I lose my pace.

I wake up in this brand new day,
trying to win the games we play,
More pressure seems to take control,
tension explodes away all of my goals.

I wake up in this brand new day,
hoping for good fortune as I pray,
More stress seems to conquer hope,
dwindling my confidence so I can't cope.

I wake up in this brand new day,
wishing that my losses will repay,
More confusion seems to always replay,
halted again I just can't make headway.

I wake up in this brand new day,
keeping loyal to my plans today,
More difficulty seems to always spread,
struggling along so I can't get ahead.

I wake up in this brand new day,
building up dreams on what I say,
More barriers I just seem to face,
stumbling over so I lose my pace.

I wake up in this brand new day,
striving for man kinds peaceful stay,
More news headlines reveal society,
as we try hard everyday, to fight anxiety.

" the dole " copyright by steven morehu davies,
completed 13th august 1994.

Low income, narrow budget, hoping to make ends meet,
old fashion, empty pocket, system pushing you to cheat,
Four walls, car repairs, kids stuck home, no outing,
overdue bills, final notice, flying words, feeds shouting.

Welfare grant, shop account, trying to hide bloody shame,
evil hearts, kick starts, selfish stallers at their game,
No headway, lost respect, survival getting times
tougher,
lotto dreams, horse track, whole family stands to suffer.

Colour brochures, showy display, window shopping just a
tease,
bus shelters, wheels rolling, no pushchairs jump in
please,
Food bank, pawn shop, use peters to pay paul,
rocket rents, power supply, high costs break the law.

Court fine, time payment, struggling to carry heavy load,
ashtray butts, black tea, tensions high boom explodes,
Auto payments, service fees, ripped accounts in the fire,
hangover downs, pull backs, accusing each other the liar.

Un -occupied, lost esteem, use the next save a dollar,
unemployed, dead goals, guilty plead yes your
honour,
Legal aid, blood test, disqualified licence
conviction,
drug highs, suicide, temper breaking point
addiction.

Budget advice, alcohol council, pressure relief from more
booze,
home violence, paddy wagon, friction feeding hard
abuse,
Marriage breakdowns, court orders, one sided stories to
be told,
divorce papers, child custody, life,s hidden secret, the
dole.

" breath of life " copyright by steven morehu davies,
completed 7 december 1996.

City air was my first breath of life,
it has to be told there is no other way,
This city air full of anxiety and strife,
I think the wind told me just the other day.

It has to be told there is no other way,
this city air full of disturbance and stress,
I think the wind told me just the other day,
yes, this city air has just become a mess.

It has to be told there is no other way,
this city air full of agitation and rush,
I think the wind told me just the other day,
yes, this city air has just become to much.

(chorus)

Country air, where have you gone,
Country air, where did we go wrong,
Country air, where have you gone,
alone on your own is where you belong,
Country air, where have you gone,
give me the air to sing this song.

It has to be told there is no other way
this city air full of confusion and pain,
I think the wind told me just the other day,
yes, this city air just drives me insane.

It has to be told there is no other way,
this city air full of frustration and strife,
I think the wind told me just the other day,
yes, this city air was my first breath of life.

" the lonely wanderer " copyright steven morehu davies,
completed 3rd january 1998.

The cathedral stands solemn true,
in the gloom of the misty square,
The early morning broom sweeper,
alone with no voices heard anywhere.

A homeless wanderer drifts in,
near empty wine bottle in his hand,
Unshaven and drawn in face,
drenched coat covers holey shoes in sand.

Black tom cat trails in season,
low tails whisk off around the bend,
Church bell hangs high and solid,
no angel message yet to send.

Shattering of the smashed bottle,
he searches a picked up tattered purse,
Fumbling for some hope destiny,
he swears out a drunken mumbled curse.

(chorus)

He just wants to be alone,
He's just the lonely wanderer,
His life is now poor,
His life is now so unsure.
Where he's going,
He does not know anymore,

He's just the lonely wanderer,
He just keeps on searching,
He just keeps on roaming,
He just keeps on thinking of her.

Beneath the historic oak trees,
he snores his breath away,
Maybe that odd red sunrise,
might open dreams of a brand new day.

Pattering footsteps quickly disappear,
disturbed outcry somewhere in the dark,
Tree tops sizzle in full alert,
flashing colors reflect towards dim park.

The old man bends his knees close up,
camouflage covers his drifting bed,
Silence settles down once more,
disruption captures a glimpse of sky red.

Un-reality exists in forever sleep,
the first downtown bus sqeaks as it arrives,
Office workers scatter their ways,
the old man wonders if he is still alive.

He stumbles and raises to his feet,
dirty coat wipes his story lined face,
Head bowed slowly through society,
he drifts on to find another lonely place.

" the fallen leaf " copyright by steven morehu davies,
completed 4 august 2001, chorus 27 may 2012.

Like the wild turmoils of one's life span,
to the delicate brisk of springtime breeze,
Through the turbulence of the hurricane winds,
I hold my youthful days with all my ease.

Like the un-for seen curses of frozen blizzard,
to the ever changing seasons of life's pages,
Through the sudden drought of heated waves,
I hold my hot angers and my moods changes.

(chorus)

You are my ancestry, you are my whole birth,
you are my offspring, you are my whole earth,
You are my losses, you are my forgivings,
you are my whole life, you are my whole living.

I show you respect, and I live my whole life for you,
These are the things, I will give all for you,
I'll show you my heart, this song we will sing,
the things I will do for you, is my everything.

Like the tender buds of new growth birth,
to the spreading veins of patterned green,
Through the aged story lines of imperfection,
I hold my brittle paleness within the blending scene.

Like the frailness of ones quickened lifespan,
to the now withering after the seasons show,
Through my happiness and my suffered trails,
I lose all strength, and now I gradually let go.

" the ones that can tell " copyright by steven morehu
davies, completed 10 sept 2018.

I know all of your hurts and pains all so well,
only sufferings in this old broken world of hell.

It hits you real hard when it all happens so fast,
simple things in our life are the things we don't ask.

It is all too sudden and never thought they would fall,
simple things in our life are the things we can't ignore.

It is only the demons at work to affect the old mind,
simple things in our life are the things we can't find.

It is up to the only one if the soul wants to go,
simple things in our life are the things we don't know.

I know all of your hurts and pains all so well,
only us who have been there, the ones who can tell.

" no red letter year " copyright by steven morehu davies,
completed 26 november 1996.

It's been no bright no red letter year,
has been right from the very start,
I've been worn, I've been torn,
been struck by a lethal shark.

It's been no bright no red letter year,
been cut up from the stories I'm told,
I've been obsessed, I've been depressed,
been shoved out into the cold.

It's been no bright no red letter year,
everyday I live with pain and hurt,
I've been down, I've pushed around,
been pushed down into the dirt.

It's been no bright no red letter year,
bogged down in this bloody mire,
I've been cheated, I've been mistreated,
been burnt down by your fire.

It's been no bright no red letter year,
living this life of devastation and hell,
I've been confused, I've been abused,
been cursed by your cold spell.

It's been no bright no red letter year,
bogged down in this bloody mire,
I've been cheated, I've been mistreated,
been burnt down by your fire.

It's been no bright no red letter year,
living this life of devastation and hell,
I've been confused, I've been abused,
been cursed by your cold spell.

It's been no bright no red letter year,
living my life has been so untrue,
I've been raged, I've been encaged,
i've been on the verge of suicide fear,
I have cried, I have died, and it's all because of you.

Full of fear, bloody no red letter year,
Full of fear, bloody no red letter year,
Full of fear, bloody no red letter year. . .

" maturity of age " copyright by steven morehu davies,
completed 11 june 2007.

Life's like a crawling, slimed, cobra in it's readiest,
symbolic, reception,
life's like a raising, vibrating, rattler in it's deadliest
hypnotic, deception,
Life's like is so untamed, intimidating and fearless in it's
deathliest venomous sway,

But as for us, life will become wholesome, solemn and
righteous,
when itself becomes it's sacred message of today.

Life's like a statued, rearing, stallion in it's towerful,
staging, curiosity,
life's like a charging, storming, unicorn in it's powerful,
raging, furiously,
Life's like is so untamed, instigating and relentless in it's
wildest stampeded gait,
But as for us, life will become full-bodied, treasured and
prosperous,
when itself becomes it's destiny fortune of fate.

Life's like a speeding, racing, hyena in it's willing survival,
progression,
life's like a stalking, prowling, panther in it's killing
revival, obsession,
Life's like is so untamed, accumulating and heartless in it's
prancing frustrated mood,
But as for us, life will become harmony, peaceful and
tranquil,
when itself becomes it's spirited wisdom of shrewd.

Life's like a scheming, bludging, user in it's antagonising,
demanding, manipulation,
life's like a jealous, guilty, conman in it's demonising,
slandering, accusation,
Life's is so un-controlled, murderous and gutless in it's
paranoid hideaway rage,
but as for us, life will become holy, perfected and eternal,
When itself becomes it's virtuous maturity of age.

" just yesterday " copyright by steven morehu, completed
28 december 1994.

Life's been to easy, life's been so hard,
it was learning just yesterday,
today I have turned up the worried card.

Life's been so kind, life's been so mean,
it was loving just yesterday,
today I hate everything I have ever been.

Life's been pure joy, life's been true pain,
it was spiritual just yesterday,
today I am disturbed crazy to the brain.

Life's been a blessing, life's been a curse,
it was heavenly just yesterday,
today I have grown disorderly worse.

Life's been real smooth, life's been so rough,
it was gentle just yesterday,
today I can not cope and just had enough.

Life's been in faith, life's been betrayal,
it was loyal just yesterday,
today I am leaving behind a revengeful trail.

Life's been in control, life's been disorder,
it was calm just yesterday,
today I will sell my soul for destructive mortar.

Life's been true peace, life's been pure hate,
it was harmony just yesterday,
today I will kill the future to devastate.

Life's been so good, life's been real bad,
it was living just yesterday,
today I am trembling down on disturbed mad.

" root of all evil " copyright by steven morehu davies,
completed 11 august 1994.

Money !, So powerful, turns this big world around,
oil states, huge cities, third degree uncivilised towns, Gold
bullion, paper money, never to be at fault,
millions dying, cannot cope, rising skyscrapers, bank
vaults.

Nine to five, global pullution, just another wider whole in
our sky,
oil spills, gold mining, wildlife left there to die,
Prime country, man invation, pulp paper to build a new
town,
endangered species, rain forests, more trees are cut down.

Hearts treacherous, selfish greed, imperfect desires of a
real man,
bank balances, growing larger, too busy to give you a
hand,

Shanty towns, over crowded, non existent in many eyes,
wall street, stock markets, out to cut throat the next guy.

Land peasants, tough survival, then along came lucky
fortune,
forgotten roots, puffed pride, I'm gonna fly away to the
moon,
Vanished escape, running away, travelling away fast from
the poor,
i've got this, I've got that, don't wanna know you no more.

(chorus)

Money, it hurts you, it changes you, then suddenly it's got
wings,
money, it guides you, it wins you, over powerful,
mysterious things,
Money, it brainwashes you, it grabs you, gets mould in the
brain,
money, it cons you, it controls you, then it stabs you with
more pains.

Concrete jungle, showy display, riches never felt so great,
greed's seed, selfish gains, brotherly love or just pure hate,
Food shortages, unemployment, anxiety stirs up as bullets
shoot,
satan's empire, kingdom ruler, the love of money, the
hidden root.

" armageddon " copyright by steven morehu davies,
completed 27 november 1996., original 1982.

The calming sun has disappeared, along with the warm
beautiful day,
casino's are jambed packed, cold hearted bitches looking
for pay,
The aristocrats and the loan sharks, their money buys
more power,
it's a strike jackpot !, bingo !, could this be another lucky
hour.

Fearsome wind gusts and thunder, warning down
destruction as it blows,
heavy rain's and giant hailstones, the freezing ice and the
deep snow,
Darkened skies turning jet black, lightning strikes out it's
blinding light,
earthquakes and tidal waves, coming into celebrate for
the night.

Earth shaking with a raw vengeance, the power supply is
blacked out,
when is this fear going to end, yelled the bankers widened
mouth,
Screaming woman and glamour diamonds, the filthy and
the poor,
chandeliers swaying in wild motion, money machines
smash to the floor.

(chorus)

Yes !, I am the almighty !, with the power and the glory !,
yes I am here,
I have come down to take my faithful followers in my right
hand !,
Yes !, I am the almighty !, with the power and the glory !,
yes I am here,
I have come down to destroy all evil throughout the land,
Yes !, I am the almighty !, with the power and the glory !,
yes I am here,
I have come down to give this new earth in my will !, as
the promised land.

Devastation by holy judgement, not one wall will be left to
stand,
awesome revenge and raw bloodshed, by the almighty
god's very hand,
Total chaos is in live session, ultimate power and vast
control,
shattered life and dreaded confusion, death marking up
higher toll.

Sheer panic and enraged terrors, lights flashing out it's
red danger,
there are no escape doors here today, for this is my great
day of anger.

" when I'm insane " copyright by steven morehu davies,
completed 24 july 1995.

Treat me just right, treat me just fine,
I can't take being upset all the time,
Treat me real nice, treat me real cool,
I can't take being called a fool.

Treat me real happy, treat me real love,
I can't take being disturbed up above,
Treat me real joy, treat me real peace,
I can't stand being disturbed underneath.

Treat me real gentle, treat me real heart,
I can't stand being ripped apart,
Treat me real warm, treat me real good,
I can't stand being misunderstood.

Treat me real calm, treat me real choice,
I can't take it when I lose my voice,
Treat me real soft, treat me real kind,
I can't take it when I lose my mind.

Treat me real careful, treat me real whole,
I can't take it when I lose control,
Treat me real lovely, treat me real snugly,
I can't take it when I turn ugly.

Treat me real smooth, treat me real tops,
I can't take it when I can't stop,
Treat me real special, treat me real tender,
because I can't take it, when I can't remember.

Treat me much better, treat me right again,
cause I can't take it when I'm insane.

" rags to riches " copyright by steven morehu davies,
completed 5 january 2019.

I was tired of the same old anxious rigged up marole,
The pain and the anguish of the mind, body and soul,
I was thinking of a way to set down a newer dream,
The pain and the anguish is what it all has seemed.

I was sick of the spirit that hurt me all over before,
The pain and the anguish of being drunk on the floor,
I was anticipating about the life set before me ahead,
The pain and the anguish is what my heart has bled.

I was scheming of the ways to forfeit all of the cold bills,
The pain and the anguish of good fortune is my true will,
I was wondering about the way to rid the hurt and strife,
The pain and the anguish is what has toiled my whole life.

I was desiring of the joys of living glamour wealthy,
The pain and the anguish being drunken unhealthy,
I was bored with the struggles of making ends meet,
The pain and the anguish of others calling me the cheat.

I was wishing of the karma would turn around the tide,
The pain and the anguish of the things I can not hide,
I was trying so hard to but ended on the wrong path,
The pain and the anguish tolling and all that I hath.

I was hoping for the heavy burden to change my whole past,
The pain and the anguish of always ending up being last,
I was praying for the long journey to remove all torn stitches,
The pain and the anguish to will power, my rags to riches.

" the joker " copyright by steven morehu davies,
completed 27 november 1996, original 1981.

They call me the joker, what's yours ?,
I already damned know, I know it for sure,
Queen, king or jack, I'm higher than all,
I'm the man in black, now it's your call.

Just play your cards, and play them neat,
now it's your start, so don't try to cheat,
Just play your best, don't make it hard,
or I'll leave you left, out there in the dark.

Just play your game, and play it right,
or I'll leave you lame, without a fight,
Don't mess me around, if you wanna play,
cause I'll come down, and you will pay.

(chorus)

They call me the joker, I'm higher than all,
I've seen many cheat, lying on their call,
They call me the joker, I'm higher than all,
I've seen many in defeat, and I've seen them fall.

All the kings and queens, rules and things,
Rings and circles and everything,
Can't fool me, I'm the joker you see.

I'm the man with the frown,
the man with the shrewd smile,
Whenever I come down,
I will defeat you with style.

I'm the man with the laugh,
and who laughs the longest,
I will hold back until last,
I will defeat the strongest.

I'm the man who won't lose,
the man is the odd stranger,
I conquer whoever I choose,
I will defeat you in danger.

I'm the man who will survive,
The man who masters poker,
I must win to stay alive,
And they call me the joker.

" the joker in the pack " copyright by steven morehu
davies, completed 4 december 1996.

Just play your hand, and play your call,
cause I'll make my stand, so don't try to flaw,
Just play your cards, and play your highs,
cause I'll come down hard, so don't try to lie.

Just play your game, and play them neat,
cause I'll leave you lame, so don't try to cheat,
Just play them steady, and play your bet,
cause I'll come down ready, so don't try to forget.

Just play your blacks, and play your lead,
cause I'll come and attack, so don't try to mislead,
Just play your reds, and play your stake,
cause I'll leave you dead, so don't try to fake.

Just play your ace, and play your king,
cause I'll show my face, so don't try to fling,
Just play your queen, and play your jack,
cause I 'll come down mean, so don't try to stack.

Just play them right, and play your deal,
cause I'll come and fight, so don't try to steal,
Just play them shrewd, and play your money,
cause I'll come down rude, so don't try to be funny.

Just play them cool, and play your stuff,
cause I'll come down cruel, so don't try to bluff,
Just play them hot, and play your sight,
cause I'll take my shot, so don't try to skite.

Just play them smart, and play your half,
cause I'll tear you apart, so don't try to laugh,
Just play your kind, and play your pack,
cause I'll come down blind, so don't try to slack.

Just play your trump, and play your suit,
cause I'll make my jump, so don't try fluke,
Just play your kitty, and play your pool,
cause I'll show no pity, so don't try to fool.

Just play your will, and honour your poker,
cause I'll play to kill, and they call me the joker,
Just play for your life, and honour your call,
cause I hold the knife, and you will surely fall.

Just play your guest, and honour your attack,
cause I am the best, the joker in the pack.

" the new world " copyright by steven morehu davies,
completed 22 july 1995.

See the magnificent stars flicker out her shining brilliant
twinkle,
See the colorful rainbow release out her proud shower
sprinkle,
See the drifting clouds pass over the still moon of silent
isolation,
See the glitter sun shine gold onto all of earth's global
population.

See the splendid tree expose out her high silver rayed
beams,
See the grand waterfall as fallen leaves float on
downstream,
See the grinding wheel spin as it the squeaky windmill
then stops,
See the draft horse stride hard to plow the meadow
supply crops.

See the dawn horizon as the freedom melodies awake to
sing,
See the peasant hand milk to feed her young growing
offspring,
See the dusk sunset as it gradually disappears over the
seas,
See the soldiers letter as the distressed mother drops to
her knees.

-------------------- Steven morehu Davies --------------------

See the eruption thunder burst ferocious clouds clashes
out wild,
See the wise man's long beard as he teaches wisdom to
the child,
See the thrashing waves raise up her victory midnight sea
spray,
See the lonely alcoholic scavenge food for his old dying
birthday.

See the tranquil waters reflect the warmth romance
summer heat,
See the honeymoon cruiser as the sunken battleship rusts
beneath,
See the wedding couple walk the church aisles to swear
their vows,
See the shadowed veil as they mourn over old age funeral
bows.

See the rain forest echo laughter as wildlife kill to survive,
See the crowd confusion waiting on the royal carriage to
arrive,
See the festive celebrations as military march in mighty
victory,
See the wartime rubble as the innocent are disturbed to
misery.

See the atomic explosion as it sprays nuclear radiation
over miles,
See the contaminated farmers death bed fearing to live a
longer while,

See the stock market crash as a squatter lies dead on a
greedy power joke,
See the redundant labourer stumble home as his dreams
go up in smoke.

See the botanical gardens as the autumn leaves contrast
the peaceful park,
See the emergency sirens as the rape victim lies
unconscious in the dark,
See the floral archway as the retired judge prides his
garden paradise,
See the atheist critic persecute the jehovah witness in
blasphemy despise.

See the bridge monument as the city lights speckle in
background delight,
See the glamorous mall complex as the back alleys shade
murder of the night,
See the proud sky tower as the restaurant revolves in
casino style fashion,
See the royal empire as news headlines feed affairs of
private passion.

See the homosexual priest as he preaches true contrary to
last night,
See the millionaires mansion as they bet and gather for
the big fight,
See the mental health patients daily addiction of brain
control intake pills,
See the legal lawyer negotiate payment on a forged
document sole will.

See the industrial empire pump toxic pollution over new
construction,
See the fault line crust shatter enormous towers down to
destruction,
See the spectacular fireworks as jesus christ died for us at
the stake,
See the party decorations as the little girl puts hot flame to
her cake.

See the tourist complex as they sunbath on a black russian
cocktail straw,
See the ghetto slums murder their neighbor for a simple
apple core,
See the clock chime as rush hour speeds up the confusing
sands of time,
See the abandoned child begging to a wealthy foreigner
for a tiny dime.

See the lightning volts stretch out her fork flashes down to
the earth,
See the medical alert as the teenage mother labor cry's to
give birth,
See the explosion lift off as the billion dollar project blasts
off into space,
See the dying refugee straining to cover her starving
newborn babies face.

See the senile war veteran forgotten in his isolated world
forever,
See the marriage bond shattered when the symbolic gold
ring said never,

See the playful children not knowing one day the boy will
chase the girl,
See the new birth baby crying as it is joyfully welcomed to
the new world.

" the refugee " copyright by steven morehu davies,
completed 6 august 1994.

People crying and human dying,
No fresh flowing, crystal clear, grand waterfall mountain,
Unknown traces and lost faces,
No coloured rainbow, trickling free, display sprouting
fountain.

Dim fire lamp and squalor camp,
No nutrition, energy declining, thousands onward arrival,
Barren drought and divisions bout,
No painkillers, fatal disease, poor scrounging survival.

Mingling mope and beggars hope,
No open arms, stolen aids, dirty empty broken plate,
Crisis critical and selfish typical,
No future goals, wandering confusion, destiny price of
fate.

Stumbling aground and corpse bound,
No medical supply, decaying odor, heavy penalty of life,
Shelter scarce and emotions pierce,
No gift wraps, favourite treats, christmas cake memory
knife.

Pots plenty and bellies empty,
No candy bars, orchard trees, homemade pie servery,
Sheer desperation and vast starvation,
No love romance, wine or dine, tender candle anniversary.

Bible text and drained breast,
No family table, purring cat, contented warm log fire,
Salvaged scraps and times elapsed,
No more willpower, hopeful prayers, another poor life has
expired.

" the unknown hour " copyright by steven morehu davies,
completed 5 march 1995.

When is the flaming fires going to descend then burn
down,
When is the giant hail going to smash over the whole
ground,
When is the tidal waves going to bash over the sea shores,
When is the shaking earths going to erupt with its huge
roar.

When is the deep thunder going to strike out deafening
loud,
When is the volt lightning going to thrash through the
clouds,
When is the warm sun going to withdraw away it's bright
light,
When is the soothing moon going to vanish from the still
night.

When is the heavy ground going to open up its earth's
crust,
When is the heavenly floods going to burst forward then
bust,
When is the hurricane winds going to gush out with cold
fear,
When is the brilliant stars going to display then disappear.

When is the damned transformers going to explode out
it's flash,
When is the mighty landmarks going to topple over then
crash,
When is the earth ruiners going to expire out into it's
doom,
When is the darkened days going spell out it's death
gloom.

When is the great babylon going to powerfully self
destruct,
When is the world governments going to ever peacefully
instruct,

When is the hour glass going to hurl vigorous sands at our sight,
When is the anger of god going to heave out his justice might.

When is the sheep and goats going to be lined up for seperation,
When is the confused swords going to attack out in frustration,
When is the dragon's tail going to rampage out it's violent hiss,
When is the graveyard tombs going to raise from the abliss.

When is the wild kingdom going to tear out into the dead flesh,
When is the birds of heaven going to feast at the leftover mess,
When is the proud castles going to crumble back to old stone,
When is the saved righteous going to pick up all the left bones.

When is the four winds going to let loose all of its stored power,
When is the holy prophesy going to prove out it's last hour,
When is the heavenly powers going to reveal its final revelation,
When is the all evil to be wiped out with gods almighty devastation.

" imperfection " copyright by steven morehu davies, completed 8 january 1998.

We are good, we are bad, we are happy, we are sad,
We are short, we are tall, we are big, we are small,
We are dumb, we are clever, we are surprised, we are never,
We are slow, we are fast, we are forwarded, we are last.

We are untidy, we are dressy, we are spotless, we are messy,
We are dull, we are delighters, we are depressed, we are blighters,
We are humble, we are haughty, we are righteous, we are naughty,
We are excused, we are easy, we are clean, we are sleazy.

We are cunning, we are shrewd, we are pleasant, we are rude,
We are selfish, we are sharing, we are treacherous, we are uncaring,
We are blameless, we are needy, we are generous, we are greedy.
We are callous, we are mild, we are mature, we are wild.

We are interesting, we are humorous, we are exciting, we are serious,
We are reluctant, we are secure, we are certain, we are unsure,

We are stalled, we are minded, we are seekers, we are
blinded.
We are adaptable, we are cool, we are careful, we are
fools.

We are hopeless, we are useful, we are denial, we are
untruthful,
We are gifted, we are pampered, we are spoilt, we are
hampered,
We are fortunate, we are malice, we are lucky, we are
jealous,
We are vigorous, we are pills, we are healthy, we are
killed.

We are active, we are lazy, we are energetic, we are hazy,
We are keen, we are unsure, we are dodgers, we are lured,
We are goals, we are dreams, we are occupied, we are
seems,
We are sober, we are intoxicated, we are reality, we are
instigated.

We are redundant, we are payed, we are employed, we are
delayed,
We are distorted, we are clear, we are alert, we are
unaware,
We are shy, we are open, we are reserved, we are broken,
We are quiet, we are chatters, we are loners, we are
shattered.

We are unknown, we are special, we are homeless, we are wrestled.
We are different, we are ashamed, we are experienced, we are blamed,
We are genuine, we are fakes, we are assertive, we are mistakes,
We are wealthy, we are poor, we are noticed, we are ignored,
We are neutral, we are flirts, we are hermits, we are hurt.

We are weary, we are wise, we are affectionate, we are despised,
We are educated, we are used, we are praised, we are abused,
We are understanding, we are careless, we are stubborn, we are relentless,
We are stumbled, we are changed, we are idlers, we are disarranged.

We are exceptional, we are curious, we are determined, we are dubious,
We are original, we are admired, we are discouraged, we are uninspired,
We are misunderstood, we are invincible, we are upright, we are terrible,
We are humiliated, we are higher, we are loyal, we are liars.

We are popular, we are reserved, we are respected, we are nerved.
We are compelled, we are attracted, we are enticed, we are distracted,

We are leaders, we are observed, we are workers, we are undeserved,
We are cherished, we are cheated, we are favoured, we are mistreated.

We are tutored, we are choosers, we are directed, we are losers,
We are tested, we are styled, we are promoted, we are trailed,
We are professional, we are investigation, we are amateurs, we are imitation.
We are advanced, we are retarded, we are academic, we are downhearted.

We are debaters, we are insistent, we are willing, we are resistant,
We are organised, we are overstated, we are dependant, we are underrated,
We are injustice, we are laws, we are perfectionists, we are flaws,
We are unlawful, we are corrected, we are illegal, we are infested.

We are criticised, we are elevated, we are commended, we are relegated,
We are disastrous, we are inventive, we are oriental, we are offensive,
We are consumers, we are peasants, we are civilised, we are non existent,
We are imaginative, we are devoted, we are strategic, we are cut throated.

We are unknown, we are special, we are homeless, we are
wrestled,
We are drifters, we are home, we are together, we are
alone,
We are settled, we are immigrants, we are law abiding, we
are ignorant,
We are united, we are isolated, we are families, we are
separated.

We are deserted, we are adored, we are abandoned, we
are unassued,
We are refugees, we are announced, we are ghettos, we
are denounced,
We are hated, we are loved, we are lectured, we are
shoved,
We are silent, we are quarrels, we are orderly, we are
immoral.

We are modest, we are attractive, we and sextual, we are
inactive,
We are impatient, we are commanding, we are contest,
we are demanding,
We are emotional, we are charmed, we are tender, we are
harmed,
We are delicate, we are obscene, we are affectionate, we
are mean.

We are fornicaters, we are desired, we are frustrated, we
are expired,
We are engaged, we are renewed, we are unfaithful, we
are untrue,

We are atheists, we are achievers, we are persecuted, we are unbelievers,
We are married, we are remorsed, we are widowed, we are divorced.

We are superior, we are minimal, we are christians, we are criminals,
We are deceived, we are undisputed, we are lifesavers, we are executed,
We are fortunate, we are relieved, we are suicidal, we are grieved,
We are protected, we are escaped, we are confined, we are raped.

We are volunteers, we are nurturers, we are pioneers, we are murderers,
We are peaceful, we are pain, we are rulers, we are insane,
We are prosperous, we are friendly, we are enemies, we are envy,
We are soldiers, we are ill, we are parents w are killed.

We are trusted, we are betrayed, we are respected, we are slayed,
We are civilians, we are disarmed, we are liberated, we are harmed,
We are actors, we are awarded, we are veterans, we are unrewarded,
We are victory, we are eliminated, we are conquerers, we are devastated.

We are wanderers, we are flocks, we are searchers, we are
shocks,
We are children, we are adults, we are flesh, we are faults,
We are young, we are soul, we are blood, we are old,
We are honoured, we are memories, we are remembered,
we are cemeteries.

We are imposters, we are bled, we are forbidden, we are
misled,
We are preachers, we are generations, we are offspring,
we are temptations,
We are created, we are winners, we are conceived, we are
sinners,
We are glory, we are crying, we are healing, we are dying.

We are privileged, we are outcasts, w are future, we are
past,
We are marriage, we are life, we are death, we are strife,
We are spiritual, we are society, we are important, we are
anxiety,
We are cursed, we are blessed, we are holy, we are
obsessed.

We are imperfect, we are people, we are godly, we are
evil,
We are false, we are true, we are human, we are you.

" hello and goodbye " copyright by steven morehu davies,
completed 9 march 2005.

If you visit my doorstep,
and I do hear your knock,
I would be gladly obliged,
and to pleased to unlock,
But I would appreciate first,
if you would simply just call,
Because I won't open up,
to a maybe stranger at all.

If you can understand,
Weather it's day or the night,
I would be gladly obliged,
and there be no boogie fright,
But I would appreciate first,
without any fuss or case,
Because I won't open up,
I simply can't see your face.

If you can only be polite,
And just call out your name,
I would be gladly obliged,
and there's no one to blame,
But I don't know who you are,
and what the hell I should say,
then ! you can bloody bugger off,
And best be on your way.

" the midnight butt stroller " copyright by steven morehu davies, completed 10 february 2019.

This morning, I am out there on the street again,
trying to satisfy my desire to calm the pain,
Frustrated again with the toils of life today,
frustrated again with the problems of low income pay.

This afternoon, I am out there on the public seat again,
trying to satisfy my integrity to calm the pain,
Frustrated again with the toils of life today,
frustrated again with the problems of low income pay.

This evening, I am out there on the avenues again,
trying to satisfy my dignity to calm the pain,
Frustrated again with the toils of life today,
frustrated again with the problems of low income pay.

This night, I am out out there on the footpaths again,
trying to satisfy my anxiety to calm the pain,
Frustrated again with the toils of life today,
frustrated again with the problems of low income pay.

This month, I am out there on the street gutters again,
trying to satisfy my society to calm the pain,
Frustrated again with the toils of life today,
frustrated again with the problems of low income pay.

This year, I am out there on the street lights again,
trying to satisfy my royalty to calm the pain,
Frustrated again with the toils of life this rockin roller,
frustrated again with the problems striving the midnight
butt stroller.

" not leaving me with death " copyright by steven morehu
davies, completed 8 august 1993.

You're the hardest thing, I,ve ever tried to fight,
been my closest friend, through the loneliest night,
Too many long years past, I'm so addicted to it,
my body screams out loud, don't you ever try to quit.

I'll give it up tomorrow, I know time will show,
tried many times since, that was so long ago,
I'll do it all next time, that's what I always say,
but you're still in my hand, every single a day.

When there's nothing to do, too much spare time,
I reach straight for the packet, and a glass of wine,
I sit down and I think, what else would I do,
I think I'll go damn crazy, if it was not all for you.

(chorus)

I got to run and blow, got to let you know,
I got to shiver and show, got to let you all go,
I got to scream and shout, got to throw you about,
I got to do it all now, I got to throw you out.

One more after another, I do take you for granted,
you're so close to me now, can we ever be parted,
I've taken so much of you, now I'm losing my breath,
trusted you my friend, you are not leaving me with death.

" the contented bottle " copyright by steven m davies,
completed 19 june 1995.

Self satisfaction, self relief best,
self pleasures, and ultimate test,
Self rewards, self worth,
self relaxation, and ultimate curse.

Self habit, self uncontrol,
self routine, and ultimate tolls,
Self sorrows, self unreality,
self tensions, and ultimate pity.

Personal downers, personal highs,
personal setbacks, and ultimate cries,
Personal problems, personal drinks,
personal trouble, and distorted think.

Pure abuse, pure insane,
pure sufferings, and ultimate pains,
Pure obsession, pure spells,
pure depression, and ultimate hell.

Sheer confusion, sheer intoxication,
sheer stress, and ultimate frustration,
Sheer mistreated, sheer blinded,
sheer cheated, and disturbed minded.

Ultimate bottle, ultimate sessions,
ultimate indulgence, and ultimate lessons,
Ultimate adultery, ultimate throttle,
ultimate sinners, and the contented bottle.

" just one beer " copyright by steven morehu davies,
completed 27 september 1999.

Just a relaxed smoke and a chilled iced beer,
here's a toast to my cobbers of goodwill cheer,
The thought of the taste of smooth bitter sweet,
this should quench down well in this scorching old heat.

Maybe just one more drink for the good old road,
into the drifting spree of the cool scenery mode,
Just give me one of those sturdy wide old mugs,
the next round I'll shout us just two more jugs.

Just another virgin packet of tailor made smokes,
so much to say to all of the laughing old blokes,
I can't resist that brewed bubbled frothed head,
should have been headed homeward to my good old bed.

Just make that whiskey a straight out stiff double,
been such a good night without a peep of trouble,
What time does the old nextdoor liquor store close,
I'm feeling so fine and I've forgotten all my old woes.

Back at home with a full brand scotch on the label,
making a racket with half empty glasses on the table,
Forgot about my neighbours trying to sleep nextdoor,
blacked out stoned drunk and cold asleep on the floor.

I can't remember anything about that row lastnight,
I can't remember anything about that stupid old fight,
I don't remember the police even calling back in here,
I only went out for a quiet ciggy and just one beer.

" quiet drink " copyright by steven morehu davies,
completed 12 january 1995.

Sunshine outing, beach towel, suntan lotion, picnic
weather,
barbecue aroma, energy children, leisure time, family
together,
Vanilla ice cream, spicy sauce, open invitation, freedom
space,
social mix, laughter play, groovy fine, happy face.

Mellow spirit, chatter talk, cigarette lighter, funtime burst,
soothing music, tape replay, song selection, quenched thirst,
Radio station, bitter beer, unwind down, conversation,
freezer ice, coruba rum, melody tunes, anticipation.

Table drummer, acoustic strummer, musical flair, unique voice,
dancing pair, talented duo, classic hits, harmony choice,
Scotch whiskey, smoker pipe, mingling folk, frenzy crowd,
heavy rock, modern rap, speaker volume, double loud.

Wasted high, druggy daze, seduced pass, rocking beat,
shaking loose, spotlight view, loose conduct, raged heat,
Flirting arms, drunken pash, over indulged, hotstuff trick,
stumbled stroll, bloated burp, toilet seat, spewing sick.

Unshaven mask, crashed asleep, party session, rowdy night,
empty crate, shouts erupt, shattered glass, drunken fight,
Noise control, midnight call, security lights, final warning,
obscene language, verbal abuse, disturbed neighbour, dusky morning.

Nightclub travel, carload squeeze, overcrowded roam, hitting town,
driving bliss, checkpoint stop, boys in blue, flagging down,
Licence check, breath test, vehicle keys, confiscation,
finger prints, photo flash, holding cell, police station.

Excess limit, custody remand, court hearing, intoxication,
guilty pride, stubborn hate, empty stomach, recuperation,
Sober reality, night recall, confused mind, blotted think,
drinking habit, end destination, alcohols curse, quiet
drink.

" still I seek it some more " copyright by steven morehu
davies, completed 27 june 2002.

See those staying a long time with the wine as god's word
has forewarned,
the gluttons and the drinking will end with poverty and
mere rags of torn,
See the woes and the uneasiness the result of over
droused thinking,
the contentions and the unconcern are the dark pits of
heavy drinking.

See the red wine exhibit it's tempting maturity of deep
bloody colour,
the first taste leads in turn to a well deserved enjoyed
another,
See the red wine sparkle as it's primed age is well served
with ready quickness,
the crystal glass is partaken with a keen will and devoted
slickness.

See the earthen vase gradually empty with the slow
dullness of the eyes,
the disrespect and the greediness will leave you wounded
with covered lies,

See the red wine exhibit it's firery blood like the lethal
venom snake,
the strange visions and violent words of an uncontrolled
mans mistakes.

See the vases broken apart with the bad rivalries of a wild
mans drunken rage,
the loose conduct and the immoral lusts leads me
frustrated and enraged,
See the shattered vases devastation as the morning open's
it's revelation destruction,
the venomous bite struck and has smitten me but to no
memory or reconstruction.

See the mixed wine exhibit it's deadly colour like a sharp
eyed stalking sniper,
the end bite of the serpent satan and it's secreted poison
of the devils viper,
See the distorted wine exhibit it's dulled colour as I
stumble on through the door,
the end result of over indulgent, yet I don't awake and still
I seek it some more.

" so confused " copyright by steven morehu davies,
completed 8 february 1998.

Inside my head I'm so confused,
I seem to live within fright and abuse,
I try to believe the nextdoor voices I hear,
I can't work out if its real or clear.

Inside my head I'm so confused,
I seem to hear the same message oozed,
I try to understand the waves and shouts,
I can't work out what it's all about.

Inside my head I'm so confused,
I seem to distort more whenever I booze,
I try to piece together the private calls,
I can't work what they want me for.

Inside my head I'm so confused,
I seem to suffer setbacks and so I lose,
I try to piece together all the secret clues,
I can't work out what I'm supposed to do.

Inside my head I'm so confused,
I seem to be lost in which way I choose,
I try to have control as I painfully learn,
I can't work out which way I should turn.

Inside my head I'm so confused,
I seem to get distressed instead of soothed,
I try to picture this joining jigsaw effect,
I can't work out why it's all so indirect.

Inside my head I'm so confused,
I seem to desire proof of self losed,
I try to face this unknown world all alone,
I can't work out if I can do it on my own.

Inside my head I'm so confused,
I seem to notice her forever bluesed,
I try to cope with the whole curiosity lot,
I can't work out if I should try it again or not.

Inside my head I'm so confused,
I seem to sense the other man accused,
I try to push ahead from being so slow,
I can't work out if I should run or go.

Inside my head I'm so confused,
I seem to only rely on only self assumed,
I try to go over on only bare words they say,
I can't work out if I should just leave or stay.

Inside my head I'm so confused,
I seem to be lost in which way to choose,
I try to believe that I could be famous someday,
I can't work out if I should just go over today.

Inside my head I'm so confused,
I seem to recognise something is luring true,
I try to strengthen as I play confused cards,
I can't work out why something easy was made so hard.

" conceivement forever " copyright by steven morehu
davies, completed 14 april 1995.

I am looking straight into you,
you know it all quite well too,
Staring eyes of crystal blue,
I stare straight back again into you.

You turn back around towards me,
roving eyes so honest and free,
Natures attraction lurng key,
future visions of family tree.

Our eyes are dazed so far away,
arched up high rainbow arrays,
Stargazer of dreaming displays,
leaning waves of soft meadow hay.

(chorus)

You attract me again today,
you attract me again always,
Your attention is displayed,
your direction is portrayed.
I need to be safe inside of you so true,
you say you want me all around you too,
You say you need my seed, I understand,
you say you want me as your loving man.

Looking again back straight into you,
wonders of courtshipping clues,
Sextual desires so brand new,
instincts have told me timings true.

Constantly we both start to blush,
hot blood is flowing it's rush,
Flashing lights, our senses do flush,
lips whisper out, saying darling hush.

Waiting to descend back down to land,
soothing calm words of soft bland,
Bonds say join together, we understand,
then I slowly take your warm hand.

Now I am your man deep down inside,
caress feelings we both can't hide,
You're now my woman truth confide,
our love is turning over the tide.

Your panting now begs for my all,
kissing your signs of command call,
Rhythm burning our friction together,
natures warm exploded out agenda.

We can't take sweet anymore,
released climax's history score,
Making love now, it's so true together,
a new life now, conceivement forever.

" Just call me " copyright by steven morehu davies,
completed 13th october 1996.

Please call and just tell me where you are,
tell me today if you have gone away very far,
Say to me that everything is just so alright,
please call me soon on the telephone tonight.

Please don't you go out with another man,
Come back tonight and hold my lonely hand,
Help me honey to carry this old burden along,
come back and tell me hon just what went wrong.

Please call and take away this hurtful cold spell,
I want you to know that I've been worried to hell,
Simply call and tell me that it's not the final end,
come back home to me and be my only true friend.

(chorus)

Just call me, so that I know that you love me instead,
just call me, I think I'm going right out of my head,
Just call me, so my groaning heart can rejoice,
just call me, I just need to hear your sweet voice,
Just call me, so that my drained soul can delight,
just call me, so that I can sleep on through the night,
Just call me, and take away all of this cold pain,
just call me, just say you are coming back home again.

I'm so confused cause I really miss you so true,
I just want you to say that you also miss me too,
I just can't handle this dreadful striking pain,
I need you to call me and just help heal my brain.

I'm so longing to be your man deep inside,
I've got to have you near close back by my side,
I am truly going completely out of my dull head,
please just call me and come back home to our bed.

I'm so lonely, please call on the telephone right now,
help me to cope with this raw situation somehow,
This is cutting so deep into my hurting cold heart,
please call, and we'll both strive to make a new start.

Please call, and say you remember all of our heart plans,
please call, and say that I'm still your only true man,
Please call, and say that you have always loved just me,
the first time I met you, I knew our love was meant to be.

So just call me dear, I know many times I was wrong,
but in our arms together is where I truly belong,
Every time I hear a shudder I will jump up for a peep,
but I will wait for you still, and can't fall back to sleep.

" back into my life " copyright by steven morehu davies,
completed 15 april 2001.

My eye's dazed out wide, like the full moon in it's
illuminating solemn trance,
my body was motionless, like the statued stallion, in it's
victorious stance,
The day you reached out, and wildly slammed that old
cottage door,
I saw the giant willows weep, when they gently brushed
the earth's dim floor.

My mind flashed out bright, like the blazing lightning
striking out of all's it's control,
my heart beat was raging, like the bullfighters red cloth
taking it's furious toll,
The day you stepped out, and left me shattered and
devastated in raw shock,
I saw the turbulent cold ocean, when it crashed against
the lonely jagged rocks.

My hands shook frantically, like the rustling of the
rattlesnake raised at deadly ease,
my brain waves were buzzing, like the anger of the
interrupted busy hive killer bees,
The day you walked out, and smashed our smiling photo
clear off the lounge wall,
I saw the skies turn to black, when the whole earth jolted,
in it's thunderous call.

My nervous system ceased, like the unsteady roots of a
giant kauri tree,my knees wobbled hopelessly, like the
first steps of a new birth foaled pedigree,
The day you ran out !, when you threw your gold diamond
ring towards my sight,
I saw the radiant fireballs, when the planet erupted on
this destructive Armageddon's night.

My hot blood was surging, like the downpours of
streaking sulphurs and red fires,
my soul was immobilised, like the lost Antarctica with no
more life willing desires,
The day you stormed out, and you forgot that engagement
photo of a dedicated loyal wife,
I saw the mighty powers of heaven, when you left me and
suddenly you came back into my life.

" silver dream " copyright by steven morehu davies,
completed 8 december 1996.

A silver dream like a northwind,
could have never come true,
Cause there was no clue,
of what to do.

So we stopped for awhile,
in a creepy little aisle,
But there wasn't any style,
until we gave it a trail.

So we all got curious,
and started getting furious,
That if we wanted a career,
it could be very near.

So we all sat down,
and started playing around,
But we took it so cool,
and started acting the fool.

Now the years have gone bye,
we never sang our song,
And our dreams have died,
we never played our song.

A silver dream like a northwind,
could have never come true,
Cause there was no clue,
of what to do.

" castle of gold " copyright by steven morehu davies,
completed 8 december 1996.

When I was young,
out there in hot sun,
Along the golden sand,
I held my mamma's hand.

In her hand was a parcel,
inside it, a plastic castle,
Then she said, it's up to you,
son, whatever you want to do.

So I built it up high,
up far up to the sky,
And with a silver glare,
I just began to stare.

Then with a sudden rush,
my mind was flushed,
And that's when she said,
now it's in your head.

Son, if you want to live,
then you learn to forgive,
Son, because if you do,
then your dreams will come true.

I saw a golden band,
in that hot sand,
On that golden hot day
when mama took me out to play.

" civilised state " copyright by steven morehu davies,
completed 26 march 1995.

In the garden, enjoyed work, leisure time, casual pace,
melting heat, sunray beams, wiped brow, sweety face,
Self satisfaction, tidy grounds, praised words, refreshed
shade,
creative ideas, blinded flash, glitter sun, clouds fade.

Tobacco paper, cigarette toke, country aroma, scenery
green,
wonderment daze, tranquil haze, sighed relief, moments
free,
Native shrubs, children's swings, mountain view, nature's
best,
cup of tea, earnt respect, written scripture, contents rest.

Peaceful flight, butterfly flutter, melody wings, gentle
breeze,
buzzing bee, rustling leaves, whistling tunes, graceful
trees,
Tender drops, shower speckles, horison display, colour
rainbow,
gradual puddles, hailstone beats, feather flakes, purest
snow.

Political climate, parliament debate, voting election, trail
mistake,
strategy changes, opposition party, overseas debt,
inflation rate,

Global atmosphere, toxic pollution, unemployed, crime
wave state,
forest fires, brutal disasters, selfish greed, mankind hate.

Discipline decline, racial confusion, gang warfare, warrant
intrusion,
drunken bouts, family violence, street roamers, welfare
institution,
Sports stadiums, flying goals, victory roars, challenge
handshake,
out or order, riot confusion, rock concerts, forgery takes.

Gambling casinos, mortgage debts, business travel, liquor
outlets,
hollywood mansion, bodyguard hire, movie empire,
concord jets,
Disruptive war, city devastation, civilian death, prison
camps,
church worship, confession priest, un peacekeepers,
rocket ramps.

Artillery convoy, nuclear bombs, satelite spies, sunken
ships,
wildlife zoos, rat race pace, stock market crash, waitress
tips,
Pestilence tolls, refugee roam, boat people, empty plate,
earthquake convulsions, skyscraper tower, ghetto slums,
civilised state.

" planet earth " copyright by steven morehu davies,
completed 14 october 1996.

Coal mining, earned crust, dirty laundry, working labour,
hotel cleaner, white collar, office hours, perk favours,
Children's care, part timers, full employment, wage
amounts,
home maintenance, housewife duties, shopping isles, bill
accounts.

Valley machinery, construction sights, country farming
lumberjack,
skyscraper tower, underground casino, money machines,
cracker jack,
Native tradition, sightseer tours, motel complex, hotel
bars,
concert venue, limousine travel, riot rages, rocker stars.

Pedestrian crossing, lunchtime bell, school homework,
dinner plate,
school certificate, university entrance, lawyers degree,
judge magistrate,
Television shows, grandstand hats, weekly ticket, lotto
winner,
step parents, rebel teenagers, gang fortress, imperfect
sinner.

Sextual intercourse, human desires, labour contractions,
new birth,
courtship romance, marriage vows, graveyard funeral,
sunday church,

Family entertainment, babysitter hire, candlelight
anniversary, document will.
alcoholics anonymous, women's refuge, homeless
wanderer, homicide kill.

Pharmaceutical, flashing sirens, fire fighters, victims
saved,
unemployment, robbery mission, drug plantation, crime
waves,
Aged pension, war veteran, retired homes, radio talk back,
hospital nanny, crippled invalid, internal disease, heart
attack.

Shipping port, import warehouse, rail containers,
aboarded flight,
political election, parliament debate, polling booth, news
tonight,
Government deficit, stock markets, inland revenue,
inflation rate,
Welfare grant, benefit survivors, food parcel banks,
swappa crate.

Family heritage, billionaires, art collection, security locks,
rural delivery, courier jet, antique auction, postal box,
Business strategy, bank manager, austin bentley, holiday
batch,
lakeside mansion, loan interest, home collateral, urgent
cash.

Industrial pollution, carbon monoxide, global warming,
survival pay,
rising sun, dawn horizon, dusk sunset, working day,
Tornado swirls, volcano lava, earthquake rubble, nature's
curse,
still moonlight, stars at night, solar system, planet earth.

" growing child " copyright by steven morehu davies,
completed 21 june 1994.

Pitch black, silent hour, birds content, warmth nest,
kerosene lamp, dimly lit, grandpa awake, nights rest,
Spring water, trickling free, fresh up chill, early morn,
duty chores, lonely quiet, routine deeds, reaching dawn.

Cold range, oven warmth, distant chatter, stock pot,
Whispered slippers, cupboard click, porridge steam,
simmers hot,
Fireside chair, moments rest, tobacco pouch, treasured
pipe,
greetings warm, comfort words, content reply, skies are
ripe.

Rattling billy, swandri cover, distant mist, milking cow,
sweet dreams, children snooze, backdoor squeak, passing
hour,
Sunrise vision, horizon peak, display rooster, walking
crows,
yawning sigh, sleepy eyes, steel kettle, whistling blows.

Gentle touch, tender shake, enlightening mood, uprising time,
nannas voice, soft reminder, happy heart, rise and shine,
Rumbling roar, copper tank, shivers cold, cuddles warm,
chilly ice, washroom towel, brand new, days born.

School uniform, neatly ironed, served oats, homemade bread,
grandpas horse, sheepdog dash, ready departure, stomach fed,
Goodbye kiss, nannas hug, pace movement, don't be late,
waving smile, maori marae, disappearing, passed gate.

Steep decline, holiday batch, paradise spot, roadside bay,
crusty prints, melting frost, beaming trees, sunlight rays,
Winding road, tranquil lake, journey hike, walk awhile,
hill destination, tarseal climb, service stop, breathless mile.

On board bus, relation blood, inside cramp, chattered full,
country ride, orderly sense, behaviour watch, golden rule,
Lakeside school, arrival fog, steep heights, testing climb,
marbles galore, shoe hopscotch, ringing bell, melody chime.

Gather draft, homework book, seated still, presence call,
lyric songs, acoustic guitar, maori culture, midget football,
Gloomy skies, indoor lunch, milk supply, playful class,
downpour rain, heavy hail, water heater, defrosted glass.

Harmony flight, breathtaking view, afternoon miss, bye today,
cloakroom coat, leather bag, puddle splash, dividing way,

Home direction, tramping track, home awaits, hours past,
nannas greets, surprise applaud, schools over, haven at
last.

Crossword book, window table, heated room, fire burning,
grapefruit tree, sugared sweet, vitamins chilled, daily
returning,
Lake jetty, group diving, peaceful walk, activity farm,
bareback ride, arabian horse, danger moments, natures
harm.

Freedom space, jam bucket, berry picking, plum trees,
lambing season, hay baling, hive attack, honey bees,
Secret hideouts, boys town, tree houses, exploring wild,
country life, adventure mind, deep memories, growing
child.

" monarchs in the yard " copyright by steven morehu
davies, completed 6 april 2000.

Just flickering through the warm springtime breeze hours,
amidst the pink petals of the wild rural stemmed flowers,
Calmly flickering briskly above her so joyfully to and fro,
settles a close encounter of displayed orange coloured
glow.

Kneeling beside lavender fragrance among daisy relation,
she reaches out to touch this pretty arrayed flickered
creation,

Her pony tails crowned in daffodils like the purest of
cream butter,
a sudden gust then grasps it's wings up into swift freedom
flutter.

Counting withered dandelions of her broken chained
maze,
waving branches dance sparrows at her sad twinkling
gaze,
The dwindling creature fades further towards the blinding
sun,
warm tear drops roll down her innocent cheeks one by
one.

Her best friend just flew away like a kind of angelic
mother,
only wanting to admire at it's striking marveled bright
colour,
She wonders why something so beautiful can be so scared,
the little girl is left lonely and tender broken hearted
instead.

Snapping off a stem she studies it in a tired curious wee
rest,
she hugs the newly white speckled plant against her warm
chest,
Wandering on home sobbing through the tall straw
wheaten grass,
gently she places it into a soil and watered filled
earthenware vase.

Calendar of busy country school routine has now quickly
sped,
walking from the dusty bus stop a butterfly appears
overhead,
Memory returns of lavender fields and it seems fondly so
hard,
strolling through the gate, appears a thousand monarchs
in the yard.

" rainbow freckles " copyright by steven morehu davies,
completed 7 february 1999.

The striding footprints slowly crunch,
towards the foggy lakeside early morn,
like a pale old miniature whale boat,
appearing vaguely in the misty dawn.

Resting beneath the pohutukawa tree,
on it's wooden and painted faded side,
bush mountains surround tranquility,
where calm mirrors exist no rising tide.

A pair of lonesome oars sleep aboard,
in a close bonded and longed devotion,
warmed gloves soon unite them again,
between a gentle knocking rhythm motion.

101

His beard hardens in the briskly breeze,
as he shrugs to shield away chilled frost,
drifting out into reflecting moonlight,
the beginning of patience and silence is lost.

Like the drone of a million crickets,
the roller reel spins out unwinding sounds,
disappearing into deep cave waters,
unsure if this tiny lure will ever be found.

Floating adrift amongst whispering steam,
he glimpses view of a small boat shed batch,
spreading bright circles of rippled silver,
pinpoints seasons hopeful mystery catch.

The fishing rod rests a little while,
clenched firm between his trembling knees,
he tucks away his suede tobacco pouch,
his sneeze reaches high into distant trees.

Softly through the giant ranges peaks,
a curious morepork makes it's humble call,
piercing through the whistling winds,
a wild stag bellows out so proud and tall.

Quickened tugs send a shivered nerve,
the nylon quivers his numb and loosened palms,
the little dingy jerks in sudden jolts,
surprise wonders within uncertain calm.

Splashing up in joyous dancing glory,
displayed in a mist of fresh showered speckles,
the horizon sun then blinds the waters,
as it glitters his handsome rainbow freckles.

" the gold treasure chest " copyright by steven morehu
davies, completed 22 february 1997.

The wide goggles are finally gradually placed,
like an awkward wobble the foot ware flapped,
on the stern edge of the wet sea explorer,
his face exposed naked and sorely chapped.

On his nose covers the airtight mouthpiece,
salt water strikes out in it's violent splashes,
oxygen bottles pulls his body downwards,
turbulent waters hitting the deck in thrashes.

Bursting bubbles rise up like thinning mud,
into the unknown world below he disappears,
like a lost alien in foreign enemy territory,
in brave courage he descends without any fears.

Entering into the below black mystery deep,
high sunray beams fades deep into the dark,
strange specimens so scary unpredictablc,
brushing his shoulder warns the predator shark.

The flashlight flickers through the misty gloom,
clenching his life saving wrist compass disk,
the awesome vessel like a tired haunted wreck,
he gradually explores depths at his own sole risk.

The silent seafloor turning into murky bleak blind,
the leisure dreams feels so dreadful frightening,
the spiked lobsters eyes shine out illuminating bright,
the giant moray eel flashes away like second lightning.

In the mad frenzy of the lethal tails motions,
agitated volted whips of the uncovered stingray,
the disturbed sediment slowly settles beneath,
where the rusted hull of the old timeless ship lays.

Through the narrow corridors of her dephilated ruins,
he searches the creatures castles of daring dare,
gently brushing against the surface floor sands,
reveals cargo artifacts of gems priceless so rare.

Hidden within her uneasy freezing dilapidation,
objects protrude likened to sharp metal blades,
the morays giant head again turns to confronts him,
winding tail lashes quickly away into the dim shade.

Her timeless presence spooks over him in fright,
he shivers as an un welcomed foreign guest,
the enormous stingray flusters, suddenly vanishes,
clearing waters then sparkles the gold treasure chest .

" grandmothers photo " copyright by steven morehu
davies, completed 11 july 2002.

Wandering near broke through the streets he observes a
glamour of the hot Las Vegas night,
on the luxurious forecourt arrives a limousine of the
purest non blemished white.

Outward perception of pure extravagance reveals a
healthy lifestyle of the filthy rich,
bowed attendant opens the doors elegantly for the
aristocrat diamond cladded bitch.

Entering the vast detailed marble complex onto the
lavishing red plushed piled carpet,
property investor confidently paces the exquisite interior
to splash her generous evenings bet.

The struggling wanderer trails in behind her with only
chance odds and imitation wishful dreams,
spectacular arrays dazzle out flashing colours from the
multitude of game pokie machines.

Glittering entertainment directs him towards an unknown
planet of endless openings to discover,
inside his tattered old wallet conceals a treasured photo of
his beloved late grandmother.

Behind it she had written- 'for you my child with the best
of luck and my loving affection',
bingo sounds jingle about constantly from the gold
stairway to every congested direction.

He discreetly reads her comforting words again with a
paused and sentimental mourned face,
in her fondest memory he slowly bows his head in a brief
distressed but saddened grace.

Her last written words ended saying 'Your good fortune
will come when you need it the most',
at a coincidental glance the flashing screen had read,
'Now the lady wishes to propose her toast'.

He places her photo beside the coin slot then captures the
figure of available jackpot win,
he inserts his last few coins as the rolling dials madly start
rotating over it's spins.

Alert sirens blast out instantly as the jingling coins pours
endless piles of galore,
as he crouches to shovel up his over spilt windfall her
photograph lies smiling up from the floor.

" the bond key " copyright by steven morehu davies,
completed 15 july 1991.

The day has now come,
when we begin the bond,
The bond of union,
that used to lie beyond.

The ring is the symbol,
that unites us with trust,
On this path that we walk,
we will carry with us.

Holy spirit from above,
there to cherish always,
Always to grow stronger,
cause it is warm from today.

May we do what is right,
may we knock at the door,
The door that will open,
where the pain is no more.

The road now behind us,
is disappearing in time,
Times of laughter and pain,
when the sun did not shine.

We can say we have something,
we can say that we care,
For now we have the ring,
that we both have to share.

We can say you are mine,
we can say it forever,
For we have started this time,
cause we are now bonded together.

We can say you are mine,
we can say we now are free,
This is until the end of time,
as we now earn't the bond key.

" hey mum !! still the best " copyright by steven morehu
davies, completed 30 October 2015.

Hey mum !, You are well known to be the woman, the
strongest one of us all,
you carried us all through, and to me, you seemed to
never surrender and fall.

Hey mum !, You will always leave a memory, that will
always stay strong in our hearts,
there will never be another to come into our life, to do evil
and then tear us all apart.

Hey mum !, You gave us all the joy, the joys of all of our
endless precious life,
whenever I was searching, you dragged me back out
againfrom all my worries and strife.

Hey mum !, I will never forget when you told me, you have
to be cruel to be kind,
I thought it was sounded really harsh, I never saw wisdom
because of being so blind.

Hey mum !, You taught me to grow up hard, and you
taught me to grow up real strong,
whenever I was depressed, I would remember that you
would always sing to a song.

Hey mum !, You were born from a chief, the youngest
beauty from that time on,
there will always be that gift, the gift you left us way back
then and many years beyond.

Hey mum !, You would always talk about our Blackmore,
and to play 'Catch the Rainbow',
whenever I do play it , I do recognize, that you were a big
part of the colorful show.

Hey mum !, I thank you for your experiences, and you gave
me your blessed dollars,
I was only being myself at the time, and my fond love for
you grew more and more stronger.

Hey mum !, I remember the old days and wild parties, and the good old 'purple' sounds,
whenever you ever do leave us alone here, your presence will always still stay around.

Hey mum !, This is from your eldest son Tipene, and from us all who arrived here today,
that you will always be somewhere there, and all your photos will be showed and replayed.

Hey mum !, May you still remain content and humble, you battled through life's ultimate tests,
just to say hi to you again, the only one, our Karaoke queen, hey mum !! still the best.

" jimmy (jocks) james " copyright by steven morehu davies, completed 27 march 2012.

This treasure is all for you, to our very own sacred James,
of course we will miss you, and you will never to be any blame,
If you did decide to do that, and chose to take your own life,
I believe you were hurting, in mixed up confused mental strife.

Wish you had of opened up more, to all of us all around,
we spent so much time together, with our musical sound,
Going to miss your gentle company, that will last on for
years,
when I woke you in the mornings, you never showed any
fears.

Everytime I look outside my door, at your lonely old seat,
I think I still see you there, and it feels quite special and
neat,
You will never leave us my son, and always proved that to
me,
you were such a giving boy all the time, and all of us could
see.

When you used to rap to that music, I thought you were
just a gun,
little did I realize at the time, that was your escape and all
of your fun,
Maybe we should of taken more notice, of the sickness you
faced,
but we all know deep down, that you can never ever be
replaced.

There is so many things, that I want to say for you today,
but it's too hard to remember, all of those deep
yesterdays,
When we had our drinks, seemed to start with 'smoke on
the water',
so many times it was you, dad, susan and shell, my dearest
daughter.

All I know that I kept telling you, about dad and maybe the powerball,
I can not comprehend that you had faith, and that you did fall,
The things I will find so hard, is that it was never to be a sin ,
that I can not share it with you anymore, if should I ever win.

All I know now son, is that your heart has gathered us all together,
because your distant portray and memories, will affect us forever,
As I expressed before son, you suffered mentally and never to blame,
from us all here today, always our intelligent jimmy jocks James.

" my dear michelle " copyright by steven morehu davies,
completed 20 april 2012, perfected 16.

This is a poem and a song all for you my daughter michelle,
I have been wanting to write this for years and I know this so well,
Whatever hurtful trails in the past was not meant to be that way,
the feelings built up is what I would like say to you every day.

You have been and proved all your close love for your dad,
I know all these emotions because it leaves me feeling so
glad,
You took care of jimmy jocks and lewis cause it's in deep
in your heart,
even the family all know you were always very kind from
the start.

Dad has many original talents you realize it's hard to find,
I am saying this to you because I know I can be just so
blind,
You sacrifice and persevere to give out many gifts of
cheer,
you make my day when you arrive when I am having my
beer.

Please don't you cry whenever you think of words in the
poem,
that's what you may tell your friends if they get to know
him,
I guess dad is very quite unusual in an out of it sort of a
way,
but I am not perfect and also make my mistakes many a
day.

Mum and dad did struggle but you always had food on the
table,
when you were little you and jimmy seemed to be just so
able,

We tried our best to raise you three under all those
circumstances,
but mum and dad did celebrate at night with our sing song
romances.

I do know shell is that dad has lyrics that can turn into
song,
the day I will feel proud and you know to whom it all
belongs,
This special poem is expressed to capture dreams of soon,
when the spotlight comes from deep purple into the
beautiful tune.

Dad got to the top of the world cause I suffered many a
trail,
our hit song book will then last on for many years awhile,
I write to reveal pains that we all face and touch many a
soul,
to shine a glimmer of hope and that life's stories have
been told.

We have to stride forward my dear and keep fighting this
old world,
I adore your kindness and you will always be my little
princess girl,
The day will come when we will reunite with plenty
laughter in the air,
then we will celebrate the moment when the words turn
into millionaire.

And we all know that dad has written over the long years
so well,
when this poetry is published, then it's all for us, my dear
michelle.

" my baby shontelle " copyright by steven morehu davies,
completed 18 december 1996.

My baby shontelle,
Your pretty face I won't forget,
you're the youngest of the three,
You are daddy's favourite pet.

My baby shontelle,
You never try to make mistakes,
you're so delicate in your ways,
You are the icing on the cake.

My baby shontelle,
Your tiny voice makes me cry,
you have got dads little nose,
You are the pearl of my eyes.

My baby shontelle,
Your trying heart makes me sad,
you have got dads copper hair,
You are very special to your dad.

My baby shontelle,
You are an intelligent little girl,
you pick up things so quick,
You are my rare treasure pearl.

My baby shontelle,
You were born in heavens world,
you are just a little model,
You are a pretty flower girl.

My baby shontelle,
You are so innocent and so wise,
you sing away your tender heart,
You are a star in my eyes.

My baby shontelle,
You touch my heart like gold,
you always pray up to the sky,
You are the mirror of my soul.

 My baby shontelle,
You put me in paradise together,
you have your fathers every way,
I love my baby shontelle forever.

" rarotongan josie " copyright by steven morehu davies,
completed 13 march 2019.

I went up north island to try fix up my lost old marriage,
took an airflight and things did not feel so royal carriage,
While there I battled on and I wrote 'the lonely wanderer',
It was into the long night as things became a lot longer.

I went to the liquor store to try to cope with the whole
stress,
took a lot of smoke, drink and coffee and did not care a
less,
While drinking I was worn out, anxious and plenty of
yawning,
It was so exhausting as I kept writing on through till
morning.

I went off to my old bed and I discovered I was relieving,
took on the heavy load and never knew I was conceiving,
While sleeping little shony was awakening up in our bed,
It was so out of it that I was so surprised at what she said.

I went onto the shopping centre to buy the kids a gift buzz,
took a crouch down as I turned to look and it was my cuz,
While we hugged then travelled, called in for some drinks,
It was so coincidental and couldn't believe what to think.

I went on celebrating the occasion, the things that don't last,
took a trip back to the old bay place to check my long past,
While there met this girl Jane and we became so close friends,
It was an experience and I told her my marriage had end.

I went to the craft shops with her to keep up the goal of try,
took a determined heart to keep going on to perfect my butterfly,
While we were drinking with June she told her I was too slow,
I was showing her 'so confused' and studied things I don't know.

I went back to the south island and met Sue and wrote 'awaiting arms',
took along a brand new path and she helped heal all the harm,
While five years had past I never knew about something so rosey,
I was shown a photo of this beautiful teenage girl, my rarotongan josie.

" out of it sue " copyright by steven morehu davies,
completed 7 may 2006.

I once went out and met this girl,
she's the most out of it in this world,
You never ever know just what she thinks,
then she's gone when your eyes go blink.

I once went out and met this girl,
she's the most out of it in this world,
You never ever know just what she wants,
then she's gone when you're walking up front.

I once went out and met this girl,
she's the most out of it in this world,
You never ever know just what she does,
then she's gone when you're having your buzz.

(chorus)

She's my girl, she's my only fun,
she's my world, she's my only one,
She's my angel, she makes me feel so fine,
she's my blessing, all of the time,
When we baffle, it's all understood,
everything's groovy, she makes me feel so good.

I once went out and met this girl,
she's the most out of it in this world,
You never ever know just what she plans,
then she's gone when you're trying to understand.

I once went out and met this girl,
she's the most out of it in this world,
You never ever know just what she's about,
then she's gone when you're spending to shout.

I once went out and met this girl,
she's the most out of it in this world,
You never ever know just what she's knowing,
then she's gone when you're ready and outgoing.

I once went out and met this girl,
she's the most out of it in this world,
You never ever know just what she's scheming,
then she's gone when you're left without meaning.

I once went out and met this girl,
she's the most out of it in this world,
You never ever know just what she's doing,
then she's gone when you're wine is brewing.

I once went out and met this girl,
she's the most out of it in this world,
You never ever know just what she wants to do,
then she's gone when you're living with out of it sue.

----------------------------------'Reality of Life'----Steven morehu Davies----------------------

" dear sue " copyright by steven morehu davies,
completed 7 july 2002.

Dear Sue, I always did try my warm hearted best,
you are my comfort and my only homely warm nest,
So far my heartfelt cries just could not tell a lie,
dear Sue, these written words I just cannot deny.

We have both down through life's cruel test,
you are so very different from all the rest,
Can we forgive and both give it all another try,
dear Sue, you are still special in our twin brown eyes.

My only flame still keeps burning always just for you,
I wish your tender heart still flickers on for me too,
These solemn words is what I hope me and you would do,
I only love just you, so will you still have me, my dear Sue.

" for my girl " copyright by steven morehu davies,
completed 11 february 2019.

Thought I was a born millionaire,
thought I had lots of money to share,
Thought I was a great lucky fortune,
thought I had to fly high up to the moon.

Thought I was a talent to be seen,
thought I had lots of light to sheen,
Thought I was to drive the meanest car,
thought I had to be a born superstar.

Thought I was a super player as a strummer,
thought I had lots of power as a drummer,
Thought I was a soldier and struggled for us all,
thought I had to be a survivor refused to fall.

Thought I was a nobody and so I just drank,
thought I had a big balance in my bank,
Thought I was a winner but again to no avail,
thought I had the wind blowing into my sail.

Thought I was a fulla that likes to sing,
thought I had to go to jewelers to buy a ring.
Thought I was a striver to drown away my sorrows,
thought I had to marry this pretty girl tomorrow.

Thought I was a wishing of all of those dreams,
thought I had become another loser again as it seems,
Thought I was to be a writer of fine works to the world,
thought I had to be a power poet to get money for my girl.

" Uncle Joe " copyright by steven morehu davies,
completed 23 July 1993, chorus completed 1 may 2018.

Don't you leave us tomorrow, my uncle Joe,
You know time goes so fast, I wish it went slow,
This is true because, you're a star in my eyes,
And you do it with style, and without disguise.

You're the one I remember, the very most,
Here's a glass of wine, and I'll propose a toast,
It's so very hard, when you don't want to cry,
You deserve the best, and that ain't no lie.

(chorus)

I remember the old days all so well,
Off the cool seashore bed, you picked many a seashell,
Like a true Samaritan, you again just shared it all away,
Your skill riding the coast horse,
You knew how to do it all so well,
Back then, You were always so unreal in all of your ways.

 remember the old days all so well,
Off the still old oak tree, you picked many a green leaf,
Like a true harmonica, you then whistled out a true sound,
Your skill playing to any song,
You show to us all and beyond our belief,
Back then, You were always so much laughter to be
around.

I remember the good times, so very clear,
Seems so very real, like you are sitting right here,
The day will come when, you will be set free,
So just stay the same, as you've always been.

Classic and cool, yet, you have been through it all,
It's so hard to think, that you will ever fall,
A voice of thunder comes, from deep within you,
You make the dark sky, turn back into blue.

The waters spring forth, just like a fountain,
When you sing up high, to the victorious mountain,
The talent you have, just can't be beaten,
That's what I tell my friends, If you ever meet him.

This is from scobie, squire, topan and cindo with fame,
Boy boy, wooback, baby and, all the rest that you named,
We all remember the yodel, and the steel guitar,
Signs of a real man, and a high shining star.

Your voice has meaning, when you turn it down low,
These are the things I remember, of my uncle Joe.

" dan the man " copyright by steven morehu davies,
completed 1 august 1994.

Dan the man,
May your life span, through this lifes test,
Taking heavens request, happilly onto the next,
May you be fine, through this hard time,
Taking little wine, happilly keeping in line.

Dan the man,
May you stay cool, through worldlys fool,
Taking ministry school, happilly cherishing your pool,
May you take care, through temptations snare,
Taking wisdoms beware, happilly keeping aware.

Dan the man,
May you stay strong, through imperfects wrong,
Taking the good news along, happilly singing your song,
May you stay wise, through commons lies,
Taking deserving tries, happilly taking your size.

Dan the man,
May your heart rejoice, through narrows choice,
Taking the worlds voice, that you understand,
That its for man.

" angel sue " copyright by steven morehu davies,
completed 30 march 1995.

Her shining long blond hair, her eyes of alien blue,
Inviting long tall legs, her figure made luring true,
Tender pink rose lips, shaped perfect innocent new,
Mature sweet seventeen, black rocker high heel shoes.

Frequent calling out visits, hungry tiger tight hot pants,
Man desires rise up strong, at every eye catching glance,
Hot foxy young sweet lady, connections of court romance,
Showing everything she's got, tempting picture of sexy
stance.

Hot wheels travelling on free, shack up hippy camper
style,
Scores of more trendy fashion, colour blinding with that
smile,
Turning on the steaming heat, grooving into the rock
sound,
Manhood spinning up so wild, she shakes it all back down.

She wants it all more tonite, she don't care a stuff no more,
Treats of feminine pleasure, loves attention to win a score,
Waiting on for her Mr right, someone who will just
understand,
Teasing stalkers who do chase, fast frenzy one night stand.

She don't fall in love too easy, always running on the
loose,
Wants a man to settle her down, released frustration on
our booze,

She fell in deep love with me, she will get me if she really
can,
She wants this fun handsome stud, to be her lover rocker
man.

Young face of pure honey sweet, womanhood scent is
flooding wet,
I met her on my warm travels, fortunate chances I can not
forget,
Catwalk model a the fashion star, attraction eyes of crystal
blue,
I slipped her through my fingers, and I named her my only
angel sue.

" down underground " copyright by steven morehu
davies, completed 17 december 1996, revised 10 january
1998.

At the hotel bar I stood there in line,
waiting to buy myself one more,
From behind came a stranger man,
he said 'I've seen your face before'.

This jokers face I did not know,
sub conscience I was for memory,
He repeated again the words before,
surprised I was at his certainty.

To the bar I turned to walk away,
his voice suddenly I had recognised,
Boggled I was at his encounter,
this man I knew had been disguised.

With my back to him I then sat down,
confused I was as I drank my drink,
To check his face I turned again,
his agitated mood made me think.

With him there three associates sat,
his unusual presence made me stare,
Protection bodyguards they could be,
one sussed me out as I compared.

His distressed state made me know,
go and talk since he was not far,
My mind did clear so sudden from vague,
I realised then he maybe a superstar.

To make my move I decided to go,
I turned I did for a second glance,
Vanished they had to my surprise,
I realised then I had lost my chance.

So strange it was I told my friends,
respond back I had gone insane,
That face I knew and so that voice,
to talk to him probably never again.

His recent song released thereafter,
with plans so green and crystal blue,
From the public eyes this hidden true,
written lyrics meant my star was true.

Previous chart hits I had heard before,
into China then to Australia bound,
About down under this story was told,
for the drummer down underground.

" Tom and June " copyright by steven morehu davies,
completed 17 december 1996.

I hardly knew you both at all, I only met you twice before,
I did not have a place to stay, you took me and opened
your door,
You said you had love for me, that I remind you of your
own,
I found out that this was true, and you made me feel at
home.

I have lived here awhile now, I settled down with pure
sincere,
I feel that love has bonded us, in no hurry to move
elsewhere,
You leave me alone down here, you don't interfere or
impose,
You leave me with my freedom, though we live so very
close.

You don't charge me the world, you don't cheat or cherish greed,
You teach that love is the key, you help me out when in need,
Your sister knew my mum so well, they were thick as thieves together,
I was only a child back then, but they tied up the years forever.

Tom knew my fond family so well, they used to sing all night long,
The memories have past on to me, everytime I sing these songs,
One day I'll have to leave you both, one day I'll think of all these tunes,
Maybe one day when I get rich, I'll come back to my Tom and June.

" sweet honey flower " copyright by steven morehu davies, completed 21 july 1995.

This song's for you dear, my wee beautiful one,
The pain disappears, when you fill me with fun,
Your eyes are so real, your face is so sweet,
This way that I feel, think your really neat.

My mind's in a fuzz, do you feel it well to,
I get a real buzz, when I stare into you,
Your naturally so cute, in your trendy new clothes,
Like a sweet scenting shoot, to a sweet scenting rose.

You attract me so much, you've got this busy bee,
Got to feel your touch, got to take your honey,
Beside the garden shore, you lift me up real high,
I can't take this anymore, going to take you and fly.

(chorus)

You're my rose, you're my honey flower,
You're my favourite attraction every hour,
You're my rose, I love your scent so much,
You're my favourite petal honey touch,
You're my rose, you're my sweet honey flower.

It's a melody just for you, words expressing the start,
You treasure it all too, keep it in your warm heart,
Somethings I can't hide, when it's something this true,
It's from deep down inside, and it's all just for you.

" My man Ritchie " copyright by Steven Morehu Davies,
completed 1 July 2018.

Richard and I have now been new friends for a little while,
to me, a 'man of peace' as I saw your long haired profile,
Born into our old world on October, nineteen fifty six,
becoming a mate of his is far better than any other fix.

Been a long time since graduation, 1970 at Greenfield
High,
he don't like any scams or putting hurt onto the next guy,

From Massachusetts he simply works on hard for his
bread,
touches me, I had to share your video of the homeless
instead.

Richard will be a ripe old sixty two in a few months from
today,
thanks to Linda, Riki, Shirley and Kayla for hi on his
birthday,
I am fifty six and I also dig, Supertramp, U2, Zep and our
Ac/Dc,
I will remain your friend, visit you, since into the same
music as me.

Contracting work and power tools, Bosch, Milwaukee and
Rotozip,
I congratulate you and your journey and I will toast a new
brandy nip,
I became a great writer because I feel pains on low income
penny,
what ever may be, I will continue, from a poet of the 20th
century.

Lifetime dairies, expressed for the who ever wishes to
take a look,
I will make you famous, someday when I finally publish
our book,
Writing !, always my top work and certainly refrains me
from itchy,
it all keeps me going, let's stay cool, and thank you to, my
man ritchie.

" huru and mapu (never ever surrender) ", copyright by
steven morehu davies, completed 24 february 2019.

Bought up with nanny Araiteuru beside our old sheep
farm,
so peaceful and so tranquil away from all that was harm,
Never to feel fears or to feel bad when we are all at home,
that's the way it was like, like the king on his tall throne.

Bought up with koro Te Mapu beside our old blue lake,
so peaceful and so tranquil away from all that was fake,
Never to feel down or to feel scared when we sing a song,
that's the way it was like, and the place that we all belong.

Bought up with sister Sharon beside our old tennis courts,
so peaceful and so tranquil away from all that was fought,
Never to feel hurt or to feel anxious when ever we again,
that's the way it was like, like there can never be any pain.

Bought up with brother Andrew beside our old shearing
shed,
so peaceful and so tranquil away from all that was bled,
Never to feel down or to feel anguished when we were
getting old,
that's the way it was like, and we will never ever feel the
cold.

Bought up with three cousins beside our old dining room,
so peaceful and so tranquil away from all that was
doomed,
Never to feel blamed or to feel abused when in a brighter
new day,
that's the way it was like, and we can never go the wrong
way.

Bought up with uncle Peter beside our old meeting house,
so peaceful and so tranquil away from all that was spouse,
Never to feel dammed or to feel betrayed when we all
remember,
that's the way it was like, and why we will never ever
surrender

" gardeners daughters " copyright by steven morehu
davies, completed 25 february 2019.

I was walking home one day keeping out of suffered rut,
trying to make ends meet while still picking up old butts,
On my way home I was behind this cute sexy young girl,
could not take my eyes off her, she was out of this world.

I was thinking about being tempted by gods deadly
creation,
trying to make ends meet while going through more
frustration,
On my walks I always seem to talk to myself only,
could not make any headway, walking alone and so lonely.

I was anxious because I was scammed of so much money,
trying to make ends meet while desires grew for this
honey.
On my strolls I was waiting for my benefit to come
through,
could not stop the struggles so I was still thinking of you.

I was stressed over the long years of making no headway,
trying to make ends meet while so worried for the day, On
my paths I seem to strive to have the time just to think,
could not cope with the situation and I am thirsty for a
drink.

I was frustrated inside and started burning out for more
love,
trying to make ends meet while praying hard up above,
On my journeys I was singing along to 'smoke on the
water',
could not stop thinking of this girl I named the gardeners
daughter.

" the tenderest kiss " copyright by steven morehu davies,
completed 3 march 2019.

We went to visit my dearest friend Sues mamma dear,
we went inside the state house and we drank our beer,
As we were conversing together as a united trinity,
we were playing to our music then in walked sudden
affinity.

We went to visit my dearest friend Sues mamma dear,
we went to the liquor store and it was just over there,
As we were chatting about the talk of the neighbourhood,
we were whistling to our music and everything fine
understood.

We went to visit my dearest friend Sues mamma dear, we
went ahead drinking as I could not believe she was here,
As we were talking lots of bull and getting more and more
drunk,
we were strumming to our music and this girl Donna a
spunk.

We went to visit my dearest friend Sues mamma dear,
we cruised along so out of it that things became so much
unclear,
As we were discussing to leave and to go back to our own
home,
we were singing to our music and we went on outside all
alone.

We went to visit my dearest friend Sues mamma dear,
we went to wait for a car ride and everything was running
sincere,
As we were leaving this cool girl dressed in black spoke of
miss,
we were waiting as she approached and layed the most
tenderest kiss.

" girl called jade " copyright by steven morehu davies, completed 25 february 2019.

I lived beside this young virgin maiden a pretty half cast soul,
I was getting drunk and so confused and taking up higher toll,
She was not to far away and on into through the morning light,
I think she used to listen to me singing everyday and everynight.

I lived trying to piece together something that was all so strange,
I was getting stressed out of maybe something weird prearranged,
She was not trying to get involved and I think we were both in hurt,
I think I was going real crazy and I was upset and feeling like true dirt.

I lived struggling to carry this heavy burdened load on my tired back,
I was getting so weighed down and thought maybe a wicked spirit attack,
She was not coping and I think she was strengthening up her heart,
I think this silent girl was simply just tearing herself more and more apart.

I lived through those strange voices, waves, and bazaar lip reading,
I was getting so suicidal and lost control, no idea where this was leading,
She was not mixing with others very much and I seemed much more aware,
I think I used to often look over to her place instead of to there.

I lived by myself and hurting so much because of missing my wife,
I was working part time suffering and struggling to fight all this strife,
She was building up affection I think while crying lonely in her bed,
I think through this trailing ordeal I felt that I was looking to her instead.

I lived all alone and was writing top poetry then I would sing 'don't cry,'
I was losing control and breaking apart while thinking of a reason why,
I think she was crying all the time and I was thinking of this young lady,
I think I was drawing closer then ever and dreaming of this pretty girl called Jade.

" clairvoyance " (for maria) " copyright by steven morehu davies, completed 31 may 2007.

Never to say or to tell, far too much to ever over react,
inevitably -- we do these things without touching or to contact,
Things blowing in the air, the things we all feel,
you can be united, you are equal, we can be so unreal,
this is my correspondence that is all that is zeal.

Never to do or to try, far too much to ever over befall,
inevitably -- we do these things without speaking or to call,
Things blowing in the wind, the things we all desired,
you can be specimens, you are unblemished, we can be so inspired,
this is my understanding that is all that is required.

Never to portray or to profile, far too much to ever over beweak,
inevitably -- we do these things without calling or to speak,
Things blowing in the park, the things that we all dissolved,
you can be honoured, you are respected, we can be so evolved,
this is my appreciation that is all that is resolved.

Never to express or to visualise, far too much to ever over exist,
inevitably -- we do these things without doing or to resist,
Things blowing in the hills, the things we all seem to do,
you can be special, you are privileged, we can all be so blue,
this is my respect that is all in front of me and of you.

Never to tell or to deny, far too much to ever over excite,
inevitably -- we do these things without saying or to fright,
Things blowing in the world, the things that we can all fear,
you can be gifted, you are blessed, we can be close and so near,
this is my clairvoyance that is all for duveal, Maria.

" awhina darlena " copyright by steven morehu davies,
completed 30 july 2019.

Hi to you my new friend Awhina, hope all is well,
nice to know that you love people, cause all can tell,
You are well known to be compassionate, and a family caregiver,
Seem to look after the elderly and children,
when we all seem to shiver.

Hi to you my new friend Awhina, hope all is good,
nice to know you know my ex emma, all understood,
You are respected and a peoples person,
And yes !, emma's parents so fine,
seem to give your all to the ones out of this line,
while I was busy on my red wine.

Hi to you my new friend Awhina, hope all is tuned,
nice to know you know our Piki, Tom and June,
You are so very fond to help many a folks there,
And you are a true blessed liver,
seem to be well liked and always seem to deliver,
you are so special to many, a true real giver.

Hi to you my new friend Awhina, hope all is forwarded,
nice to know you speak the bible, so all is rewarded,
You are a past sunday school teacher,
We reap the life of a good loyal wife,
seems you are a woman who takes away all the strife,   to
put the past behind and move on with your life.

Hi to you my new friend Awhina, an old friend of whanau,
nice to know that you are there, when we all let it go,
You are a speciman of the lord christ,
There to make our life more and much cleaner,
his holy wonderment makes life much keener,
he told us this, our very own cuzzy, Awhina darlena,

" ABOUT THE AUTHOR "

My great love for the art of poetry,
Poetry under the title of author/writer,
Writer under the interest of literary.

I am Steven morehu Davies, born in Christchurch, New Zealand, on the 24th of November 1961, I separated around 1995 and have 5 grown up children, my parents separated at age 5 and I was raised by my grand parents from around 5 years old on there sheep and cattle farm in the North island of New Zealand in the country side, a beautiful paradise bay called 'Otaramarae', beside Lake Rotoiti, and the families maori meeting house of the native maori people, I was raised with my younger brother and sister, my adopted maori brother and my two maori cousins, I attended 'Whangamarino moari primary school' at around age 5 where I remember showing interest in artwork and at age 8 years old in writing, I started school at 'Richmond' primary and then 'Sydenham' primary in Christchurch where I was elevated from primer one to primer three for being so outstanding clever for my age, I wrote my first song lyrics around 1975 when I was around 14 years old, and at high school I was awarded 3rd prize for my short story competition, which I wrote about the farm and surroundings, I left my grandmother and my factory job at around age 18 and traveled with my girlfriend to the South Island of New Zealand to spend time with my father who was a fisherman nearly all of his life.

I then starting traveling a lot of the country, and taking all sorts of work including labouring, factory work and seasonal fruit picking.

I carried on writing poems and song lyrics with the intention of forming a heavy rock band with my brother and a friend also a relation from 'Whangamarino' primary school, about 1985 my traveling girlfriend and I separated, a month later I met a girl at an organic gardening work course who I married in 1991, in turn we had our four children, in around 1984 I bought a set of pearl drums, which I sold I also destroyed all my writings and grew mature and fast in becoming a family man when she became pregnant with our first child and I then disbanded the band movement.

In around 1995 I completed a business course and as a result, 'poetry' was one of my selected three work titles, I then keenly began to write again with the goal of my manuscript being published one day, during my essay I was informed that being a writer I would have to learn to except 'criticism' as many people may disagree with my writings, in around 1998 I shifted to live with my mother in Christchurch NZ where she gave me a magazine advertisement for a poetry competition, as she said that I 'must be gifted' after she had read a lot of my finished works by that time, I submitted my poem titled 'the lonely wanderer' with another twelve of my other works, as a result, it was published worldwide in an anthology called 'fire in the heart' in 1999, the publishing company liked my works so much they proposed to me to submit any poem of my choice.

I then submitted a poem I had written and completed in 1998 called 'awaiting arms' as (one of the best poems of the 20th century) about my experience in Rotorua in NZ, 1993 to 1996 of a neighboring lady that seemed to have always showed up in my life, sometimes my life has had some rather bazzar and frankly, out of it circumstances indeed, in 2006 I suspect I was attacked by wicked spirits for around 14 months solid when I attempted suicide twice and as a result ended being placed in a physiatric hospital and have been receiving medical injection for around 14 years to date, I was also attacked again around the beginning of 2019 when I attempted another suicide due to evil slander namely hearing voices, as some things in life may sound so easy, but in fact, seem so hard indeed, I had to fight so hard to produce this book against wicked spirits, but I am a willing writer of mankind at the same token, Steven morehu Davies, famous poet and lyricist.

If any person would like to request me to write a poem for you, you can contact me by writing at the following, (steven.davies.publishing@gmail.com) you can use it for whatever you like, but I will always own the copyright and I will publish the poem in one of my future editions.

I thank the readers for your time in showing interest in my writing works and english grammar acomplishments.

I will be concentrating on my 'edition two' as my next goal, may you look out for this on 'amazon. com', as I am determined to continue writing and perfecting my skills.

May god bless you in your positive endevours.
My guide rule, show and share love to all.

My butterfly invention, exterior garden ornaments, these
featured in a New Zealand road movie titled 'snakeskin',
this can be viewed on 'you tube'.

The end.

Thankyou for spending the time to read my works.

Steven morehu Davies.